Accepting Each Other

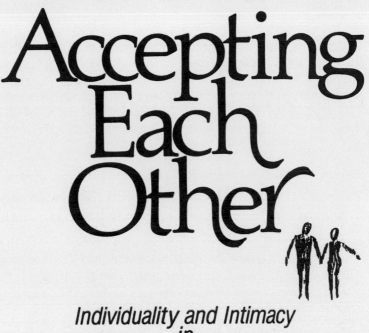

Individuality and Intimacy
in
Your Loving Relationship

Michael L. Emmons, Ph.D.
and
Robert E. Alberti, Ph.D.
Authors of *Your Perfect Right*

Impact Publishers™
Post Office Box 1094
San Luis Obispo, California 93406

Library of Congress Cataloging-in-Publication Data

Emmons, Michael L.
    Accepting each other : individuality and intimacy in your loving relationship / Michael L. Emmons and Robert E. Alberti.
        p.   cm.
    Includes bibliographical references and index.
    ISBN 0-915166-77-1 (pbk. : alk. paper)
    1. Intimacy (Psychology) 2. Love. 3. Individuality.
    4. Interpersonal relations.   I. Alberti, Robert E.   II. Title.
    BF575.I5E45   1991
    158' .2--dc20   91-22918
                                                                      CIP

Cover design by John Magee, San Luis Obispo, California
Printed in the United States of America on acid-free paper
Published by **Impact Publishers™**
POST OFFICE BOX 1094
SAN LUIS OBISPO, CALIFORNIA 93406

contents

PUBLISHER'S NOTE

This publication is designed to provide accurate and authoritative information in regard to the subject matter covered. It is sold with the understanding that the publisher is not engaged in rendering psychological, medical, or other professional services. If expert assistance or counseling is needed, the services of a competent professional should be sought.

dedication

To Kay and Deborah

acknowledgements

So many others have contributed to the ideas and form of this book, it's hard to know where to begin. Certainly the most important source of our learning about intimate relationships has been experiential: both of us are partners in marriages which have thrived for more than a quarter-century. We have Kay Seagle Emmons and Deborah Millerd Alberti to thank for our respective shared journeys, which have taught us so much.

We are grateful to the dozens of practitioners, researchers, and theorists from several disciplines whose work, colleagueship, and/or teaching has influenced our study of intimacy, and made possible this synthesis. To mention specific individuals here would surely result in leaving someone out. We believe we've identified them all in the Appendix, "Notes for Professionals."

Very helpful constructive critiques of this manuscript came from Sister Christine Bowman, Bruce Fisher, Melissa Alberti Froehner, and Marilyn Rice. Ginny Monteen provided a marvelous copy-edit of the work (and gave us honest feedback about our original title — *The Intimate Organism* — which led us eventually to abandon it in favor of the present label).

Not least among the contributors were our students and clients, whose questions and struggles gave us the motivation we needed to keep at the task.

Thanks to all.

introduction

Why do you suppose you picked up this book?

You like to read anything you can find about relationships.

You'd like to enjoy your intimate relationship more.

You're losing your attraction to your partner — or vice versa.

You're having trouble communicating with your partner.

You're concerned about whether you and your partner are really committed to each other.

You're finding no purpose in your love relationship.

You and your partner have begun to lose trust in each other.

You're trying to establish a new intimate relationship.

Or maybe you're like one of these couples:

Dan is a couch potato, preoccupied with Monday night football, Saturday baseball, "Dial-Yourself-Rich," and film at eleven.

Rebecca complains that Dan ignores her, spends no time with the kids, and avoids even the basic chores around the house.

Jennifer is seldom interested in sex, usually complaining of being tired, or observing that "all he sees in me is my body."

Mark is beginning to think it was a mistake to get married.

Samantha and Bruce have lots of friends. Bruce thinks that Sam's friend Wayne is a bit much, however. Seems that Samantha and Wayne work together, golf regularly, and have lunch once a week. Wayne is invariably invited to dinner parties at the house. . . Bruce is not just jealous, he's furious.

Sound familiar? Are Dan and Rebecca, Jennifer and Mark, Samantha and Bruce typical couples? How about you and your partner? What are the rules that govern "good" relationships? Is an "intimate" relationship really important anyway? Who makes the rules?

As practicing specialists in human growth and relationships for over twenty years, we've seen lots of Dans and Rebeccas and Jennifers and the rest. We've hurt for couples who wanted desperately to salvage crumbling relationships but didn't have the skills they needed — and didn't know how to find them. We've spent thousands of hours helping couples painstakingly piece together the fragments of marriages worth saving. And we've come to appreciate the qualities which separate successful relationships from those which are best allowed to die.

We were frustrated in our work, however, by the lack of a comprehensive model of intimate relationships. Don't misunderstand. It's not that there are no models. The professional literature of psychology and marriage counseling is jammed with ideas about how relationships work — *good*, practical, well thought-out, tested-in-practice ideas. Ideas about couples communication, about sexual relationships, about fighting. And there are some useful theoretical models of intimacy — mostly dealing with sex and/or "self-disclosure." But none of the work to date has provided a *comprehensive view of the intimate love relationship* in a form which couples — and therapists — can *use* to help a love partnership to grow and thrive.

Accepting Each Other offers such a view. This new way of looking at relationships — with a focus on *acceptance* — can be of great help to couples who are hurting and trying to save or improve their relationships. Couples like Rebecca and Sean, Jennifer and Mark, Samantha and Bruce. And couples like you and your partner. Couples who may be basically happy, but whose relationships have slipped into a semi-comfortable "neutral" gear, allowing them to coast along fairly smoothly, but without much genuine intimacy or excitement in their lives together.

For all these couples — and for you — *Accepting Each Other* presents a straightforward, practical picture of what it really takes to build a lasting and rewarding intimate partnership..

You'll find that we strongly emphasize the living, changing and growing nature of human love relationships. We want you to think of your union with your partner as a vital living *organism*. It's a new being which the two of you have created, and it's alive! It can continue to live and grow and to contribute much to your individual lives and fulfillment if you nurture it and treat it like the valuable resource it can become for you and your love partner.

We'll discuss the "organism" aspect further in Chapter Two, where we present our *ACCEPT* model of relationships. For now, let's turn our attention to the concept of "intimacy." Then we'll tell you more about this book and how it's organized, so you'll know right up front whether it's likely to be of value to you and your partner.

What Is Intimacy?

"True intimacy," writes psychotherapist Peter Kalellis, "is undoubtedly the answer to the age-old question, 'What do they see in each other?'"

"Intimacy" is a curious word. Lots of folks — including the popular press — seem to think it has mostly to do with sex. Is that all there is? Certainly not. The sexual relationship — though not unimportant! — is only one small part of intimacy. What's more, "self-disclosure" — sharing your innermost thoughts and feelings with another person — is not the whole story either. While that definition is very popular with our colleagues in psychology and other human services — and we agree that open and honest communication is a necessary part of intimacy — it's far from the whole enchilada.

"Love," says psychiatrist Aaron Beck, "is never enough." We agree, but it's not a bad place to begin! The intense emotional relationship which develops between two people who care deeply for one another's well-being has been treated shabbily in the literature of human psychology.

You and your partner "love" each other, right? And you'd like your relationship to be even better, smoother, more satisfying for both of you. In short, you want to enhance the *intimacy* in your loving partnership. If love is the *feeling* that "makes the world go 'round," intimacy is the ointment that greases the axle.

It's intimacy which takes the measure of love, which requires love to show itself, which demands that love prove itself in the day-to-day shoulder-bumping which inevitably defines a love relationship in the real world.

Yet, despite its down-to-earth side, genuine intimacy is an almost mystical phenomenon. It means opening yourself to the deepest of relationships with another person — fully trusting and accepting each other. It also is a means of growing and fulfilling yourself as a human being — more fulfilled than you might become alone. Paradoxically, it requires giving up something of yourself — voluntarily foregoing some of your independence in return for the rewards of an interdependent union with your love partner.

Complex? Yes, it is. Beyond understanding? Not really. It only seems that way if you're on the outside looking in.

The most basic characteristic of intimacy, of course, is that, by its very nature, it is shared with another person. It's an intense emotional and spiritual experience of closeness between two people who care deeply and lovingly for one another. It's more than sex, more than total honesty or "self-disclosure."

"An instrument of many strings" is the metaphor used by family therapists Howard and Charlotte Clinebell to suggest the diversity of this complex phenomenon. Their book, *Intimate Marriage,* describes *twelve* major categories of intimacy.

Intimacy is a living, changing process which exists in virtually every aspect of a love relationship, increasing a couple's happiness, satisfaction, and fulfillment. It can improve your sex life — and your communication, and your attitude, and your love for each other.

There are intimacy issues involved in . . .

. . . going to a party alone.   . . . discussing religion or politics.

. . . shopping for groceries.   . . . betting on the races.

. . . watching basketball on TV.   . . . having a drink alone.

. . . cleaning house.   . . . having a drink together.

. . . making the beds.   . . . reading a novel.

. . . refinishing furniture.   . . . working in the shop.

. . . balancing the checkbook.   . . . writing letters.

. . . buying insurance.   . . . (you name it!)

This isn't a true-false test. To the degree that you're involved in a committed love relationship, all of the situations in the list above are related to the intimacy in your life.

"What?" you're thinking. "These guys have intimacy on the brain! What does buying insurance have to do with intimacy?" It's true, some of these activities do seem pretty mundane and — on the surface — unrelated to your love for one another. But that's one of the problems. Our society has a "television view" of love and intimacy — hearts, flowers, and sex — which ignores all the everyday acts which go into a loving relationship.

We think a more comprehensive perspective will help enhance the intimate couple relationship. Here's our working definition of intimacy:

Intimacy is the loving, living bond that exists between two people who care deeply about each other. The quality of intimacy in a loving relationship is determined by these characteristics: acceptance of one another; mutual attraction, open and honest communication, commitment to the continuation of the partnership, enjoyment of their life together, a sense of purpose for this relationship, and mutual trust which honors and respects each other; individual uniqueness of the two intimate partners; and the environment in which the relationship lives.

We have agonized, fought, pondered and rejoiced over this definition. We've read dozens of others, from Webster to the full range of professional writings in psychology, marriage counseling, psychiatry — even sociology, history, philosophy and literature. We've changed our own concept often as new material, and new experiences, came to us. We had six major criteria for our definition:

- its terms had to be tangible, definable concepts;
- it had to apply to loving, voluntary, committed intimate relationships;
- it had to be as comprehensive as possible;
- it had to be consistent with the major schools of thought in relationship theory;

• it had to offer a foundation for enhancing intimate relationships.

Note that we call this a "working definition." Our model of intimacy is a work-in-progress — not a proclamation carved in stone. We hope it will be tested, critiqued, subjected to the challenges of real relationships in the real world, and to the rigors of analysis by our professional colleagues in the human services.

We also hope it will give a hand to lots of couples who are trying every day to make their relationships better.

Describing the Territory

One of the most difficult tasks in putting together a book on a complex topic is to limit the subject matter enough so it can be covered adequately in the format allowed. A book on intimate relationships can cover an incredible territory!

Psychologists and other human service professionals have done a great deal of work on various aspects of intimacy: parent-child relationships, separation and loss, narcissism, friendship, and loneliness, among others. Those subjects, while of great importance in a comprehensive exploration of the field of intimacy, are not covered in this book. We've limited our discussion to practical guidelines for enhancing intimacy in *committed adult love relationships*. (Although we believe there are many applications for the basic principles we've described.)

There are three major aspects of your intimate organism: the *environment* in which you live; the two of you as *individuals*; and the *relationship* between you. We'll be discussing all three aspects in this book, but your *relationship* itself is our primary focus.

We've come up with six key dimensions here, and we immodestly believe they provide a comprehensive framework for viewing relationships. You may think of other qualities. We believe they're accounted for within these six which form the central core of a healthy intimate relationship:

Attraction	Enjoyment
Communication	Purpose
Commitment	Trust

It may not surprise you to notice that we have offered an acronym — *ACCEPT* — which will make it easier for you (and for us!) to remember the six dimensions.

We're not playing word games here. *Acceptance* may be the single most important quality in any human relationship.

It's not possible, of course, to isolate completely any single dimension of a relationship. Everything touches everything else. How much money she earns is a factor in their happiness, as is how sensitive he is to the needs of the children. Her ability to express what she likes in lovemaking is more-or-less as important as his social skills with their friends. The six dimensions overlap somewhat, and each contributes to the partners' feeling of fulfillment in the relationship.

The next chapter describes in detail the *ACCEPT* model and its place in the system. Then there's a chapter on each of the *six dimensions*, followed by chapters on the importance of *individuality* in intimacy and an overview of important factors in the *environments* in which intimate relationships live — including families, neighborhoods, economics, and such. The final chapter offers some ideas for nurturing your own intimate partnership. An Appendix for professionals in human services covers how the *ACCEPT* model relates to other therapeutic approaches and studies of intimacy.

What to Expect from This Book

- Our principal focus is on emotional intimacy; this is not a sex manual.

- We are assuming that you and your partner are in a *committed* relationship, although not necessarily married.

We don't believe anybody has "the only" path to truth. As psychologists, we follow a pragmatic, integrative approach, drawing from the best of several viewpoints: systems, cognitive, social learning, and humanistic. ("The best," in our view, is that combination of approaches which is most valuable in dealing with the needs of a *specific* couple.)

• We advocate equality, openness, and honesty in intimate relationships.

• Our main goal is to give you the tools to help you build a stronger relationship of your own. These ideas will give you a new perspective so you can take a more objective look at your own situation.

• We are not trying to "convert" anybody, or convince you to accept our way of looking at things. We hope you like our ideas, but our goal is to help — not to sell you anything.

•The book is organized so you can "enter" it at the point which is of most concern to you. You'll find it helpful to read it all. But if you don't, you'll discover something of value in each part.

What Not to Expect from This Book

If you're one step away from seeing a divorce lawyer, this book alone probably won't solve your problem. You may still find value here — even if only for your *next* relationship! — but keep in mind that no self-help book is a substitute for professional counseling when you need it.

It is our intention to offer a model of relationship *competencies* which provide a framework for developing and improving healthy intimate parterships. We are not attempting to address the needs of those intimate couples whose relationships are significantly "dysfunctional" — in serious trouble — due to:

• severe power imbalance/inequality
• emotional abusiveness
• physical abusivenes
• chronic substance abuse or dependency (alcohol, other drugs)
• long-term disinterest in each other

- one (or both) partner's commitment to an outside affair
- serious psychopathology in one or both partners (e.g. schizophrenia, affective disorders, clinical depression, anxiety disorders)
- current crisis (e.g. discovery of an affair, death of child, financial disaster, one partner seriously hurt the other, sexual problems)
- one (or both) partner's unwillingness to improve the relationship

This is not to say that this model or the procedures we describe would not be helpful in such cases, but in any of the circumstances noted it would be important that the area(s) of dysfunction be treated by a competent therapist before attempting any significant work on the relationship itself. You'll find some helpful guidelines for finding good professional help near the end of the book, in Chapter Eleven.

How This Book Can Help You

We don't have any illusions — and we hope you don't either — that reading a book will turn your life into everything you've ever wanted. Life is not that simple. Change is hard work — especially if it involves another person as well as yourself.

As you read this discussion of intimate relationships, you'll find a new "window" on your relationship; a different viewpoint; a fresh way of looking at yourself, your partner, and what goes on between you.

You won't agree with everything you find here. Nor will all that we say apply to your situation. This model of relationships which we call *ACCEPT* is something of a theoretical ideal, worth striving for as we all try to carve out a more satisfying life for ourselves and our mates.

This book offers you a *model* of healthy intimate relationships, a *fresh perspective* on your own relationship, six *specific dimensions* to help you set goals, encouragement and reassurance about *your own options*, practical procedures for *self-improvement* in each dimension, *resources* for further exploration, and *tools* which can help you make your intimate partnership thrive and grow.

Genuine intimacy is tough to achieve, and requires the continuing effort of both partners. In this book, you'll learn a lot about how to focus your energy so you and your partner will get the most out of that effort. We believe you'll agree with us that it's worth it.

 *two*

accepting each other

A Model for Loving Relationships

If you're like most people, the words you would use to define intimacy include closeness, understanding, sex, sacredness, privacy, trust. Certainly each of these terms has a place in defining loving relationships. And there are many more. Intimacy is indeed complex — as you'd expect when you blend together two individuals, their relationship, and their environment!

Intimate relationships do have a common structure, however, and it's that structure which is described by the six-dimensional model which is the heart of this book. While each love partnership is unique in many ways, the *ACCEPT* model offers a pattern which we believe describes the key features of virtually all intimate relationships. This chapter will give you an overview of the model; later chapters explore each of the six dimensions (attraction, communication, commitment, enjoyment, purpose, trust) in depth.

Acceptance: Foundation for Intimacy

The acronym *ACCEPT* fits loving partnerships so well for two key reasons: because it labels the six vital dimensions of an intimate pairing; and because *acceptance* is such a critically important quality in any human relationship.

Self-acceptance helps you to know yourself, to learn what is important to you, to forgive yourself for "being human." (It is not related in any way to self-indulgence.) Paradoxically, behavioral scientists have discovered that self-acceptance is a necessary condition for active psychological growth. Psychologist Rian McMullin puts it this way:

"Success, love, respect, and acceptance are all byproducts of accepting myself.... Unless I accept that I am a good, worthwhile person just the way I am, I will never be happy. I am not bad, wrong, or inferior."

Acceptance of one another makes it possible to begin and continue an intimate relationship with another person. "Nobody's perfect, Dad" was a favorite defense for the five-year-old daughter of a colleague of ours many years ago. (She's now a college graduate with children of her own.) She was right, of course, and that's why learning to accept each other, imperfections and all, is basic to becoming intimates.

Acceptance of the relationship is the third element of intimate acceptance. Janice put it best when describing her beginning relationship with Jeff:

"Getting married to Jeff was like moving into a new house. You accept the house because you bought it, but it still takes some getting used to. You get better acquainted with its special qualities, like the beautiful hardwood floors or the wonderful view out back or the roomy kitchen. You have to make adjustments to things that you overlooked, like the wall in the family room that's a bit crooked, the extra room that isn't as big as you thought, the backyard that's full of tough-to-work clay. You also find that you have new responsibilities. Higher payments, upkeep, occasional remodeling are all part of the bargain."

While Janice didn't offer the corresponding details about Jeff, we can hazard some guesses. Perhaps she discovered that he was much more helpful around the house than she imagined, that he was an excellent cook, and creative in bed. But he tended to get moody and non-communicative, wasn't good with handling money, and was a night owl (she's an early bird). She may also have found that she had to adjust her schedule to include Jeff, had to take into account his dietary preferences, and she had to modify her shopping excursions. For his part, Jeff no doubt found himself adapting to similar changes as he came to accept his relationship with Janice.

Acceptance of your relationship means that you both are willing to "hang in there," to adapt, to make adjustments so the relationship can grow.

Acceptance does not mean that you throw out the need to negotiate differences. Most of us need much more practice in graceful acceptance than in negotiation skills, however.

The ACCEPT Model of Relationships

We've been promising you a closer look at the six dimensions of the intimate organism, each one corresponding to one of the six letters of the word *ACCEPT*. Let's start with a graphic view of the *ACCEPT* model, suggesting the relationship among the six dimensions and the two partners:

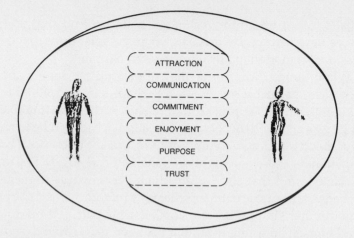

Now that you have an idea of what "it" looks like, here's that overview we promised:

Attraction What brought you together in the first place? How did you find each other — and why did you stick around? Each partner has personal qualities — personality, style, appearance, intellect, values, beliefs — which appeal to the other. These deserve continuing emphasis — long after you're hooked on each other. Stay attractive!

Communication This is the main vehicle available for creating and maintaining an intimate relationship. And despite our proud claims of having the most advanced forms of communication of all creatures on earth, we humans fail at least as often as we succeed. Assumptions, misunderstandings, silence, fear ... there are a hundred barriers to effective intimate communication, but it remains the *sine qua non* of all human relationships.

Commitment   How much does this relationship really mean to you? Commitment is a measure of your determination to hold the relationship together, how highly you value it, and how hard you'll work to maintain it. With every other dimension developed, but without commitment, a relationship will not last.

Enjoyment   Isn't this what it's all about? Having fun, enjoying life and each other, making the most of each day, taking an active part in recreational and leisure pursuits, enjoying what you do — these are the nourishment all of us need to carry us through. A vital intimate alliance gives enjoyment to each partner, and contributes its vitality to the larger community. Don't neglect your need for joy, playfulness, humor, fun, light-heartedness. Life cannot be a perpetual vacation, but you can make fun for yourself in almost any circumstance.

Purpose Purpose is a motivating force, a guiding principle which helps you define your goals and objectives, and give them direction. Purpose (or lack of it) determines whether your intimate organism works or flounders. It defines the interfaces between yourselves, your relationship, and your environment. Do you share a common view of how the world "should be"? Do you have similar views about politics, social conditions, childrearing, spiritual experiences, human life, the environment, human relationships? Can you tolerate significant differences between you in these areas? A sense of purpose is central to the success and stability of your intimate partnership.

Trust This is one of those qualities which helps differentiate intimate relationships from other human contacts. Intimate trust includes belief in your partner, the assumption that your mate is capable, willingness to put yourself in your partner's hands. To trust someone so completely that you make yourself vulnerable — opening up your deepest self — without fear. Intimate trust is knowing that your mate won't intentionally or carelessly hurt you, and will always be there when you're in need.

You may think of other characteristics of a love relationship which appear to be missing from our six dimensions. Indeed, there are two additional aspects of a love relationship which are absolutely fundamental: the unique *individual* qualities of each partner; and the many *environments* in which their relationship exists.

We found it extremely difficult to limit the list to eight factors. Nevertheless, we've found that virtually every other characteristic of intimacy is closely related to one of those, or is a characteristic of an individual partner or of the environment. We considered more than fifty such qualities in developing the *ACCEPT* model. We believe the model takes each of them into account.

Relationship As a System

We want to emphasize that the six key dimensions of intimacy, the two individual partners, and the immediate environment all interact together to form a *system*. None of the elements exists in isolation. Changes in one dimension, in the characteristics of one or both of the partners, or in the surrounding environment, will change the entire system.

Remember Dan, our "couch potato" from Chapter One? He's the incorrigible TV watcher whose partner, Rebecca, complains that he ignores her and everthing else except what's on the tube. Think for a moment about Rebecca's contribution to this process. Evidently she has tolerated it up to now, her complaints nothwithstanding. Probably she has even done a few of Dan's chores for him. And no doubt she takes care of the kids' needs which Dan avoids. Isn't Rebecca thereby *making it possible* for Dan to continue the pattern which she says she hates?

Each intimate partnership is a *system*!

Famed family theorist and therapist Virginia Satir used a hanging "mobile" to demonstrate the idea of the family system. The weight and position of each member of a family may be represented in an arrangement of wires, strings, and figures. When one part moves, it affects every other part and the entire system. Families are balanced like that, as are intimate relationships.

To make it easier to discuss the six dimensions of intimacy in detail, we've considered each separately — as if it were possible to divide a relationship into its component parts. Don't let this editorial convenience mislead you: the intimate system is *indivisible* — open, changing, growing, but *unified*. Each of the components — two partners, six dimensions, and the surrounding environment — contributes to its ever-changing shape and direction.

The system idea will come up again from time to time throughout the book — but maybe not as often or as clearly as its importance deserves. The most important times for *you* to remember "system" are those times when you're about to blame your partner — or maybe something in the environment — for something that's happened. Thinking of your relationship as a system will help you to remember that *you* are part of the problem — and of the solution.

Relationship As A Living Organism

Despite its importance in describing how relationships work, however, even the "system" idea doesn't go quite far enough. The electrical system in your car is a unified whole made up of mutually dependent parts. The plumbing system in your home, the air conditioning system in your supermarket, the telephone system in your community — lots of systems such as these function well. But they are not living, changing, or growing.

A human relationship is a *living* system — an *organism*.

Organisms are living structures, with mutually dependent parts arranged into a unified whole. All plants and animals — including the human animal — are organisms. You and your partner are two individual organisms who have come together to form a third living structure — your relationship. We believe that relationship is most accurately regarded as an *intimate organism*.

The fundamental characteristics of the intimate organism, then, are these:

- It's a unified system
- It's a living structure, growing and changing
- It involves two unique individual human beings
- It exists in — reacting to and acting upon — an external environment.

The *ACCEPT* model — viewed as a system which includes the partners and their environments — provides a thorough description of what happens in every intimate partnership. We believe you'll find it helpful as you seek to strengthen your own committed love relationship.

Our model and our ideas about how intimate relationships work have been forged in the fires of clinical experience, intuition, and the work of dozens of others in the fields of counseling and clinical psychology, marriage and family therapy, social psychology, social analysis, environmental psychology, general systems theory, psychiatry, theology, and socio-biology. (We've noted in the professional Appendix some of those who have been particularly influential to our work.)

In addition, our theoretical and clinical observations have been honed and polished personally, through long-lasting marriages to our respective intimate partners. More than a half-century of "laboratory" experience has been by far the most important contributing influence on our ideas about intimacy!

What Does Your Own Intimate Relationship Look Like?

Any given intimate organism may be pictured in terms of the *ACCEPT* model, with varying shapes and sizes of the six dimensions shown. Young couples, for example, often find that the "Attraction" dimension is of greater importance:

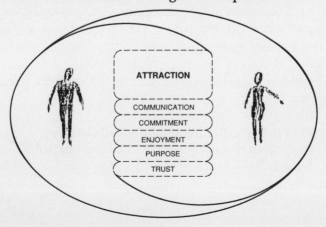

In a mature relationship, "Commitment" may predominate:

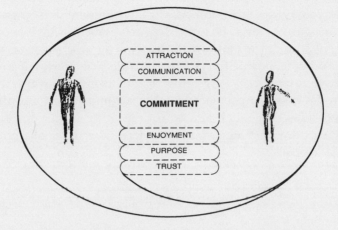

Any of the six dimensions could be dominant in the ebb and flow of a living intimate relationship. As you can see, the possibilities are many.

What does your own intimate relationship look like?

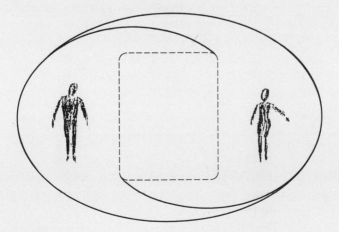

The Intimate Organism Is Not Alone!

Like all living things, an intimate organism must deal with its surroundings. The immediate environment is sometimes nurturing, sometimes hostile. Most relationships have enough internal strength to sustain themselves against short-term or not-too-strong hostile forces from outside. But a series of strong negative forces, or a long-term "siege" from the external environment, will upset all but the strongest of committed partnerships.

Picture an intimate organism swimming in a sea of environmental forces:

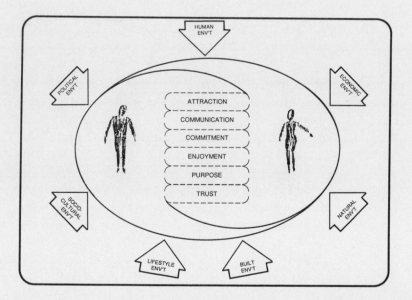

It's clear that the pressures of such factors as other people and money can be very stressful on an intimate partnership. Indeed, they can be overwhelming.

Wayne was such an environmental factor in the relationship of Samantha and Bruce. (You may recall that we met them in the

Introduction.) From Bruce's viewpoint, Wayne is a disruptive influence on his marriage, spending as much time as he does with Samantha, and coming to their home a lot more often than Bruce would like. Wayne is just one example of how environmental factors can affect a relationship. Obviously such factors can be positive as well as negative.

Keep those forces in mind, even as we direct your attention first to the dimensions of the relationships itself. A closer look at some of the key environmental influences is coming up in Chapter Ten.

Learning to Care for Your Own Intimate Partnership

The six chapters on the dimensions of intimate relationships also include some specific ideas to help you strengthen your own intimacy. Don't plan to read passively. (Even if our prose is entertaining enough to keep you interested, that's not our purpose — and we trust it's not yours either.) As you read, look actively for insights into your own intimate partnership. Apply what you learn to yourself and your partner. And find ways to improve the quality of your own intimacy.

Most couples in troubled relationships either (a) lack some of the basic skills necessary to keep their relationships growing and thriving, or (b) possess those skills but don't use them for one reason or another. We'll talk about both issues. You'll find help for building new skills and for better use of the skills you have.

Another thought on using the skills you already have. Some folks find they have good communication skills, know how to be attractive to their partners, are able to trust, etc. BUT, *when the going gets tough*, they crawl under a blanket and hide. In casual conversations, for instance, they use good eye contact, express themselves openly, ask good questions, listen well. In an argument, however, they go to pieces, forgetting everything they know about effective communication.

Such sensitive situations are an obstacle in lots of relationships, but the solution is amazingly simple: the most effective way to deal with highly emotional issues is to apply the same basic skills you use in more casual circumstances. Learn how to relax, so you can stay relatively calm when things get really upsetting. Practice good communication skills — the same ones you knew how to use before emotions escalated. Persist — don't walk away and slam the door (or your mind) shut.

Touchy situations will always be touchy, but you can make handling them easier if you'll practice the relationship-building principles described in the chapters which follow.

Growth Potential in an Intimate System

All intimate organisms are not the same, but every relationship has the potential to achieve greater intimacy, and the *ACCEPT* approach can help. As you discover new skills and insights, you can increase your acceptance of yourself, your partner and your relationship. Attractiveness to each other can be heightened, you can communicate better, have greater commitment, enjoy each other more, have more strength of purpose, feel more trust.

A particularly exciting possibility: since your intimate organism is a system, improvements in one area tend to cause improvements in other areas. If you start communicating better, attraction, commitment, enjoyment, purpose, trust, acceptance all respond in varying degrees. Anything you put into the system affects all the component parts.

Intimate systems require time to grow and change, however. Don't expect overnight improvement! Assume that change will be slow and steady; that's the wise way to view the potential for enhancement of your life together. Look at the intimate journey as a lifelong adventure in discovery and growth.

Intimacy isn't the ultimate value in life, but don't underestimate its potential to help you feel more comfortable, more self-assured, more loved. By increasing intimacy you help develop yourselves as individuals, bringing out the best in each other. And that "best" contributes to a healthier family and a more stable society — so everyone wins!

We invite you to set aside your doubts and anxieties about building a stronger intimate partnership. If you succeed, the benefits are not limited to you and your partner; the world — or at least your corner of it — will be a better place as well.

 *three*

attraction

"How Did We Get Ourselves Into This?"

Attraction is the first dimension of the intimate organism — not because it's most important, but because it's the way the whole process begins. Intimate partners begin their journey toward a relationship by being attracted to one another.

Attraction means different things to different people. Social psychologists have done hundreds of studies to try to determine the factors that draw people to one another. We'll talk about a few of the most important factors in this chapter. As you read about the ingredients that lead to attraction, think about what forms your own unique *attraction profile* and your individual *attraction map*:

• An "attraction profile" refers to the many qualities about you that draw others to you, especially those factors which attract good friends and intimates.

• Your "attraction map" consists of what *you* focus on when you're seeking a friend or intimate partner. Even if you're "swept off your feet," these qualities are in operation!

Carl Jung put it this way:

"Every man carries within him the eternal image of woman, not the image of this or that particular woman, but a definite female image. This image is fundamentally unconscious. The same is true of the woman: she too has her inborn image of man . . . . Since this image is unconscious, it is always unconsciously projected upon the person of the beloved, and is one of the chief reasons for passionate attraction or aversion."

(Marriage as a Psychological Relationship).

Jung's ideas about the "unconscious" are not necessarily ours, but the fundamental concept — that we all have preconceived ideas about an ideal mate — is very much the same.

Bill's attraction *profile* offers an example. Among the highlights: being over six feet tall, black wavy hair, a warm smile, expertise in business, a good sense of humor.

Kathy's profile has these features: easy to talk to, loves to socialize, a wonder with computers, a fine horsewoman, regular churchgoer.

The attraction *map* is the other side of the coin. We all quickly figure out someone's attractive qualities. It is as if you always have a map on the surface of your mind which activates when you meet and "check out" people like Bill and Kathy. Attraction maps are comprised of that unique mix of qualities each of us consistently looks for in a friend or intimate other. You may like blondes more than redheads; money more than personality; short more than tall; shy more than outgoing — or your attraction map may be the exact reverse!

Proximity. Psychological research has shown that a basic reason for one person's initial attraction to another is that they're in *close proximity* to each other — maybe they work together, attend the same church, live in the same neighborhood, study in the same class. Proximity leads to becoming more familiar with each other and helps them feel more comfortable. Our best friends are often those who are physically closest. Jim and Susan met in an apartment building where they lived two doors apart. Mike and Kay met in college; they lived on opposite sides of a co-ed dorm with a common eating facility in the middle. Both couples eventually married. Proximity counts!

We're always amazed to hear about couples who live hundreds (or thousands) of miles apart. More common, but still a strain on intimacy, are today's "commuter marriages," in which partners see each other only on weekends. Intimacy requires some closeness, some time together, although many couples do seem to make intimate organisms work when they must be far apart for career, economic or social reasons.

While some time together is a necessity, *optimum* togetherness is not necessarily *maximum* togetherness. Intimacy thrives on being together, but not at the expense of the individuality of the partners. Healthy togetherness *nurtures* individuality. The key — as usual — is *balance*.

Repeated exposure. This vital factor in attraction is also present with people you dislike, so there's more to the story. Repeated warm, comfortable, *mostly positive* experiences with people nearby usually lead to closeness. If the experiences are primarily negative, the most likely result is you will dislike those people. The more exposures there are, the deeper the like or dislike becomes.

Proximity and repeated exposure may not sound like real red-hot factors to include in your attractiveness profile or map — "You mean my partner and I started to like each other just because we were near each other and not too ugly?" What can we say? There is more to it than that, but these two conditions seem to be essential. Nevertheless, attraction takes place for a variety of other key reasons as well.

The following list identifies several areas people consider when checking each other out. But don't carry this list around with you the next time you're looking for friendship or romance. You're much more likely to succeed if you at least *seem* to be spontaneous!

What Attracts People to One Another?

Physical Attractiveness — Physical looks, body build, dress, athletic qualities, sexual "vibes," bodily movements, health habits.

Interests — Sports, games, hobbies, music, art, theater, nature, space.

Values and Attitudes — Relating to finances, spirituality, religion, family, sexuality, environment, work.

Intellectual Abilities — Verbal, musical, spatial, interpersonal, kinesthetic, mathematical, intrapersonal, "street smarts," book learning.

Personality Factors — Shyness, outgoingness, assertiveness, sense of humor, nurturance, tenseness, calmness.

Finances — Job security, upside potential, frugality, generosity.

Intimacy Qualitiles — Communication, commitment, enjoyment, purpose, trust.

Affection — Verbal and non-verbal expression of loving feelings, liking, caring, warmth, non-sexual touching, saying "I love you," small remembrances such as cards and flowers, going out of your way for your partner.

Similarity. All of the factors of attraction are put together in a unique way by each individual. Each of us seeks someone with whom we match up well. *Similarity* is a recurring theme in this process. You don't want someone exactly like you, but you want someone who's in the same ballpark! Opposites may attract, but similars attract more often — and last longer together. Couples typically evaluate and re-evaluate all of the attraction areas. In the final analysis, they piece together an attraction package which offers maximum mutual overall positive feelings and evaluations of each other — including a good deal of similarity.

Stephanie speaks for a lot of us: "When I met Gary, I felt that at last I'd found someone who understood me! We have so much in common, and we see the world almost exactly the same way."

As you develop a clearer idea of your individual attraction profile and map and even your *couple* attraction package with friends and intimate partners, it gets more intriguing, doesn't it? And it can be pretty complex — figuring out all the intricate details that form your unique attractiveness, how they all interact together to form a cohesive whole, and how they match up with those of another person. (If we can figure out definitive answers to these issues of attraction, maybe we'll write a new book!)

The exact patterns and reasons why people are attracted to each other still seem mystical and magical — and perhaps that's the way it should be. It certainly provides great sport for friends and acquaintances: "What does Clarisse see in him?" "Why is James going out with a loser like her?" About the best thing you can do, if such questions are bothering you, is to look over the areas of attraction noted above and try to piece together the unique puzzle which characterizes a particular relationship. Given the present state of knowledge in this field, you may be better off just scratching your head and acknowledging that there is someone for everyone. They often match up well and have positive evaluations of each other — and they probably couldn't describe the process very accurately themselves!

At the risk of ruining a little of the magic, we'd like to help you better understand this business of attraction. The following section offers a tool you may find helpful as you work at knowing yourself and your partner more fully.

Constructing Your Attraction Profile

Brainstorm and write down the components of your attraction profile. Start generating ideas of your own first. If you get stuck, use our chart on page 30 for additional ideas. Add in things that your partner and friends see as your good qualities.

Remember in elementary school when your teacher used a projection lamp to create your silhouette, then traced it and cut it out of black paper? You'll find this exercise more fun if you place your attraction qualities into a likeness of your own profile. Don't go to the trouble of using a lamp or black paper. Just draw an approximate likeness of yourself on white paper. Make it big enough to contain lots of room for you to be creative in depicting your attractiveness.

Discovering your attraction profile may be a difficult task. You have to look at yourself realistically. You're asking yourself honestly, "What is it about me that others, especially my partner, find attractive?" The exercise could bring up feelings of bragging or tooting your own horn. You might feel doubt or fear about whether you really have any qualities that you or others find attractive. You could feel slighted because you feel your partner or others don't truly recognize or appreciate some of your excellent qualities.

We ask that you suspend feelings like these for now. Focus on this as a fun exercise! Try to get into a sense of discovery. The purpose is to take a look at the *good* qualities you have to offer. Most of all, this should be a confidence and self-esteem builder. If you need to work through other feelings, you can do that later.

Constructing Your Attraction Map

Your attraction map is your inner guidance system or set of instructions for what you desire in a friend or intimate partner. It's as if you have a picture drawn in your mind that leads you to special qualities in others.

You may find it helpful to brainstorm and write out your partner's profile first. Keep at it until you can generate 15 to 25 qualities that you see as attractive. Don't worry about qualities that overlap at first. When you've finished, you can go through it and eliminate similar items.

As you start to construct your own attraction map, carefully analyze the profile you just did of your partner. Would all of those qualities be in your map? You may admire that your partner is a creative thinker, but that quality may not be in your attraction map. Pretend that you are looking for a new intimate partner. What are the qualities you value highly?

This can be an insightful exercise. First, in constructing your partner's profile you may discover traits that you had forgotten about lately. Second, you may discover that your map doesn't include some of your partner's qualities. Third, there may be qualities in your map that your partner doesn't possess.

Discussing Profiles and Maps With Your Intimate Partner

Would it be a good idea to talk about your map and profiles with your partner? Perhaps. But first, reflect on what your purpose would be. Is it constructive, to help you both work toward greater understanding and intimacy? Or is it to start a fight or to argue or to rehash longtime sore points or to suddenly blurt out secret desires. And even if your motive is entirely constructive, proceed carefully. Use good communication tools (from the next chapter). Those tools will also give important suggestions for dealing with the complexity of more difficult issues that profiles and maps might generate.

Attraction Through the Stages of a Relationship

Attraction, like the other dimensions of an intimate relationship, changes over time. What's important to you at the outset may fade as you get to know each other and fall in love with other qualities. It is possible to generalize a bit about these stages:

Early Stage. Think for a moment about what qualities first attracted you and your partner to each other. Early on, your attraction pattern is likely made up of the factors we've discussed. What catches your attention at first are the readily observable physical and emotional qualities. Fortunately, you don't have to be a "hunk" or "perfect 10," or even have that super personality that shows through in an instant! Most people will analyze more deeply and include more than the obvious features. "Howard doesn't look like Robert Redford, but the minute I met him I was intrigued. He's so intense!" That's the way Peggy put it. Whatever the reasons, this early attraction period is an exciting one. And, although these early attraction qualities change over time, their essence is always there and keeps renewing your attraction to each other.

Middle Stage. As you settle more into a committed relationship, new dimensions unfold. You discover new levels of attraction within your original perspectives. New areas of attraction also unfold as you see your partner in different settings and doing different things — working, relating to family and friends, dealing with children. Susan remembers how pleased she was when Mark actively joined her in childbirth classes before their first child was born. She saw a part of him that deepened her feelings of intimacy.

The middle stage can be dangerous as well. More depth of experience with each other may uncover problem areas that strain intimacy and dim attractiveness. These concerns may not have shown up or perhaps were barely visible in the glow of the early stage. They may be worked out through communication and acceptance, but they do have the potential to break the relationship if they aren't dealt with successfully.

Late Stage. In the late stage of relationship, the ingredients of your attractiveness profile may be faltering a bit. Age is often the dominant factor. Physical factors of attractiveness are obviously not what they used to be and the other areas mentioned above may be dulled due to age and illness. There is hope! The greying of America is on the upswing. Among the many celebs whose long-lived attractiveness actually has been celebrated are Liz Taylor, Sophia Loren, Jackie Onassis, Bob Hope, and George Burns. They're all past their youth, but — as this is written in 1991 — still attractive and full of life.

Research into other areas generally affected by aging is showing that older adults can also maintain their former levels of attraction if they take care of themselves physically and stay active and involved mentally. Even though you may falter a bit and have some health problems to deal with, your basic attraction profile remains much the same. Both partners realize that we all lose a little along the way. Yet there are still the vestiges of early- and middle-stage attractiveness. The same attraction pattern is still there to excite you, even though it may have dimmed a bit. In addition, new and exciting ingredients may come to the fore. Jan started to paint for the first time at age 65 and became quite accomplished by age 70. Our neighbor, Dr. Paul Spangler, began jogging when in his 60s and became so proficient that he won numerous races and is setting new international age-level records into his 90s! Ongoing growth keeps attractiveness vital even in the late stages of development.

Sexual Attraction

In most books about love and intimacy, "sexuality" is given star-status. Yet in several recent studies about intimate relationships, sexuality earned only second-class importance. When asked how important sex is to their overall happiness, most couples rank it below such variables as communication, under-standing, commitment. You can guess why. True sexual intimacy is an expression of all the dimensions of intimacy. In and of itself, sexuality is simply one part of attraction, and attraction is only one of the six basic dimensions of the intimate organism.

Sex is a vital part of intimacy, of course. Indeed, many folks think of them as synonymous. Although we consider genuine intimacy to be much more than sex alone, there can be no doubt that sex plays a key role in bringing — and keeping — two people together.

The importance of sexuality varies greatly, depending upon the couple. If there is no sexual relationship, an intense medium for expresing love is missing. But sex isn't the only way, or even the most important way, to express your caring for another. The old idea that "as goes sexuality so goes the relationship" is one of the major myths of intimacy. It is widely recognized among human service professionals that a successful sexual relation-ship is the *result* — not the *cause* — of strong emotional bonds.

Sexual attraction is like other areas of attractiveness —we each have our own unique attraction profile, and each of us includes certain sexuality components in our attraction maps. Good questions are, "What turns you on sexually?" and "What do you have that turns others on sexually?" Luckily for most of us, there are a wide variety of sexually attractive qualities, which can be grouped into two basic categories, *physical* and *emotional*.

Physical Attractiveness in Sexuality. Various parts of the human anatomy may be exciting to others, but there is no universal pattern. Listen to Roger: "Sharon's eyes have always been a turn-on for me. She's got big, beautiful eyes. Her lashes are natural and long. When she bats them at me I still get that old funny feeling. She also raises one eyebrow in a cute way at times when she talks. I love it."

Jackie puts one aspect of her sexual attraction to Chris in this way: "When I first met Chris at a swimming pool I admired his biceps. He worked out with weights a lot so his upper arms were big. I still like them to this day and love to touch them when we make love." Eyes, biceps, but what about legs, body hair, chests, genitals, mouths, hands, ears . . . Ears? That's right, you never know what body parts each person finds sexually attractive in others. It's nice that we are all unique in our physical makeup and desires!

Emotional Attractiveness in Sexuality. Maybe a bit more complex to figure out, but just as sexually exciting are certain emotional qualities. A partner who is shy, demure, easily embarrassed, a little naive, or "slightly innocent" turns on some folks. Others are sexually moved by partners who "take charge" or are confident, assertive, assured. The range of emotional behavior that can stimulate people sexually is as unique and varied as the physical area.

When you put the physical and emotional sexual attractors together, the picture begins to defy analysis. Nevertheless, all of us seem able to do it quite well and rather uniquely! And it seems that the composite we develop in an intimate relationship is consistent and enduring. For an outsider, the intricacies of mutual attraction of an intimate couple are beyond understanding.

Fortunately, the folks involved don't *need* to figure it out!

Suggestions for Building Attraction
- Be around your partner enough — but not too much.
- Get to know what your partner likes.
- Stay healthy, clean and fresh.
- Work hard to develop positive attitudes toward life. It's a lot more appealing than being a grouch!
- Do everything you can to improve your sense of humor. Don't be a clown, but learn to laugh at yourself and to enjoy life more.

- Develop one element in each of the areas of attraction on page 30.
- Work to improve your own attraction profile — at least those features which you can change.
- Discover all you can about your own attraction map.
- Identify the differences between your attraction map and your partner's attraction profile. Use the attitude change ideas presented in Chapter Four to help yourself *accept* these differences.
- Get to know yourself. Find out how your self-esteem or other qualities affect your attraction profile.
- Remember that attraction is only one of the six dimensions of the intimate organism, and that the relationship is a unified system. You can improve attraction by working on communication, commitment, enjoyment, purpose, trust or individual qualities.

communication

How To Talk, Listen, Solve Problems, Fight ... and Still Love each Other

Like it or not, we're *always* communicating in intimate relationships.

Think of raised eyebrows, frowns, smiles and snarls. What about head nods, stares, yawns, and sniffs? Sniffs? Yes, all of these signs — even sniffs — convey something. Deciphering exactly what the message is may be difficult at times, but communication is going on!

Words communicate myriad meanings depending on how they are said. You can say, "You're real sweet," in a warm, loving way or with a cynical zing! Words can produce hidden messages just as easily as can being silent.

Robin and Aaron were brave volunteers who showed us one of their fights in a workshop for couples:

Robin: (Glaring at Aaron and speaking loudly) "Why didn't you call and tell me you'd be late? You knew that I'd have dinner ready and the kids would be screaming! I . . . ."

Aaron: (interrupting) "Wait a minute! Hell, it doesn't happen that often. Why don't you just eat without me? If you were more organized the kids wouldn't be on your back anyway."

Robin: (volume increasing) "You never do what I want. You're always pulling something on me to get at me. You men should learn what it's like to work and be responsible for the house too!"

Aaron: (frowning, sarcastic tone) "What a thing to say. I don't know anything because I'm a *man*, is that it? *Women martyrs* do it all."

Robin: (turns away and pouts in silence)

Robin and Aaron drew a rousing hand of applause from the participants. Obviously the others recognized the pattern! Most of us get into the fray in some or all the ways demonstrated. These two certainly did a good job of breaking most rules of good communication. We'll discuss those rules later in the chapter. First, let's look at some characteristic ways many couples proceed through the stages of communication.

That Was Then . . . This Is Now

Think about your own intimate relationships and the way you communicated with your partner. Did your communication get better as you progressed from the early to later stages? To help analyze this question, let's look at the developmental stages of a "typical" couple.

Early Stage: Remember when you first became acquainted? Communication was exciting, open, spontaneous. You shared a variety of ideas, feelings, joys, concerns, beliefs, values. Things may have popped out of you that you'd never disclosed to anyone. Your goals and plans for the future, even your wildest, most far out dreams were probably an open book. That time is now often remembered as exhilarating, as if you'd taken a communication elixir which made you starry-eyed and jabber-mouthed.

Middle Stage: The luster of the early stage starts to dull a bit as the churning action of reality enters into your communication. Natural misunderstandings and conflicts arise. Assumptions and expectations rear their ugly heads. Problem areas begin to appear as the demands and stresses of living together progress. Habits, preferences, and idiosyncrasies become clearer. You are put to the test of resolving these dilemmas.

If you've developed a good sense of purpose, a capacity to adapt, and good communication skills, you can turn the adjustments of the middle stage into stepping stones to a stronger intimate relationship. If you aren't able to adapt, there will be unhappiness and perhaps dissolution. Communication either begins getting better or flounders at this stage. In the latter case, partners often use subtle-to-obvious coercion to get each other to change. If instead, communication is improved to the point that differences are gracefully accepted or resolved, intimacy becomes deeper and more rewarding.

Late Stage: If the relationship survives the tumultuous middle stage, the late stage seems to produce a mellowness, further meshing together, and working toward acceptance of each other. Many couples feel that this stage is the happiest of their relationship. The children are gone, or not around as much. There is more money, more time, more travel, and retirement is close by. Issues of health and aging loom as time moves on, but as the "stresses of striving" lift, intimate communication becomes easier and more comfortable.

Communication and The Happy Couple

Throughout the stages of a relationship, communication is the foremost means by which difficult areas of adjustment can be successfully worked out. The lighter, joyous side of life can also be greatly enhanced by effective communication. The ability to communicate cannot solve every problem, but being able to talk things out can overcome many barriers. Happy couples are largely created through communication.

Research studies support that last statement. Communication plays a central role in creating a happy, more intimate relationship. Many couple communication experts have studied the differences between unhappy/distressed and happy/non-distressed couples. Family therapists Mary Anne Fitzpatrick and David Badzinski document the importance of the communication dimensions for happily married couples by summarizing marital research findings:

Happy couples:
- resolve their problems.
- are able to express their emotions to each other.
- communicate well with each other.
- are accurate in interpreting each other's nonverbal cues.
- have more agreement and approval versus disagreement.
- make attempts to avoid conflict.
- try to reach compromises.
- demonstrate a number of supportive behaviors.
- give more positive nonverbal cues and are consistent in their use.
- are less critical of each other.
- have a higher ratio of pleasing to displeasing behaviors (than of unhappy couples).

Observers are able to document these self-reported differences in laboratory settings. The overall conclusion is that there is a remarkable difference between the way happily married and unhappily married couples communicate. Such studies point to some of the key components in making your relationship a happier one. Let's have a look . . .

Communication Steps to Happier, More Intimate Relationship

Good intimate communication doesn't often come naturally. Most of us must work at it. The balance of this chapter provides six powerful tools to help you and your partner build more effective communication:

1. Positive attitudes toward communication.
2. Basic listening and speaking skills.
3. Intimacy-enhancing communication habits.
4. Constructive thoughts, beliefs, and expectations.
5. Problem solving skills.
6. Conflict resolution skills.

Communication Tool #1:
Positive Attitudes.

The idea of a positive attitude refers to a cluster of ways in which you can facilitate your intimate communication. To obtain the most satisfying results from virtually any life activity — in fact, from life itself — it helps to approach the task with a positive attitude. Think of scuba diving with a negative attitude. Or going to a movie in a "down" mood. Or starting the day at work angry or depressed. Doesn't your attitude influence the way you respond to these situations? The same is true of your intimate relationship. But magnify the effect tenfold, because your intimate partnership is such a powerful force in your life. A negative attitude in an intimate relationship sours everything. A positive attitude helps the relationship work better and ultimately helps you both feel better.

The key components of a positive attitude in an intimate relationship are cooperation, rewarding, and patience.

Cooperation. In intimate relationships you sink or swim together. You and your partner react to each other's input (or lack of input). You can't be in a relationship by yourself. You can't solve relationship problems by yourself. You can't expect to work only on yourself and expect that to produce more intimacy. Some of your self-change will certainly help, but an intimate partnership is a mutual system. The relationship will show significant growth only when you both realize that you are intimately entwined.

The concept of "sink or swim together" has been dramatically illustrated in the field of *cooperative learning*. This approach to school classroom management — an alternative to competitive learning — requires students to work together to accomplish shared goals. Students learn to support each other, to help each other, and to encourage each other in small learning groups. The students focus both on academic material and on learning how to get along with each other. Cohesion, closeness, and a sense of "we-ness" develops. Cooperative groups foster intimacy. They also foster better academic performance as compared to individualistic learning. Educators David Johnson, Roger Johnson, Edythe Johnson Holubec, and Patricia Roy have described the process (see the Bibliography.)

The parallel to couple communication is clear. If you focus only on what *you* want and behave individualistically, your intimacy will suffer and so will your achievements as a couple. (You'll probably not get what you want, either!) By keeping the idea and practice of "sink-or-swim-together" in the forefront, your overall positive attitude is reinforced. You don't lose yourself in this process; you simply become part of a vital intimate system which pays great dividends to both partners.

Rewarding. A number of authors in the field of marital and family communication point out that behavior between partners is a product of *both* individuals. *The intimate relationship is a system!* Intimate couple behavior tends to be reciprocal in nature. Albert's unhappiness is triggered by his reaction to the input — or "non-input" — of Victoria.

Distressed couples become quite sensitive to each other's communication and will often behave like each other. Psychologists Neil Jacobson and Gayla Margolin have demonstrated this idea in studies which show that distressed couples reward each other and punish each other at equal rates. *Partners get back what they give out*, whether it be positive or negative.

Not that partners sit around and *calculate* how to behave toward each other, basing their responses on whether their intimate's comments are negative or positive. They simply learn to respond quite naturally, based on human nature and years of experience together.

The solution to the problem sounds easy. To begin reversing a negative pattern, simply start being positive. Begin talking in more positive ways. Start doing more caring *little* things for each other. Change your thoughts to a more constructive mode. Drop any nonverbal behavior that is negative in nature. Such steps aren't as easy as they may sound, but with a little practice the results may seem like magic. Both of you will start feeling better and behaving more positively.

Patience. Paradoxically, we often try to attain this vital quality through impatience! People want patience, but want it right now, this instant, immediately! Nature is slow and patient. We humans want quick fixes and fast changes. We appear to have grown out of sync with the natural way of things. The fact is, the way to become patient is through behaving patiently!

Intimate couple communication often fits the impatient model quite well. Partners operate on the idea of immediacy, wanting each other to change on the spot. It sounds like this: "If you would stop nagging me (now!), everything would be fine!" or "If you would start being nicer to me (this instant!), we could be much happier." Intimates may lose their patience and demand quick responses — "Hurry up!" "Do this!" The implied threat is that if you don't react *now*, you will suffer the consequences.

In their pursuit of fast change, many partners resort to force. In an attempt to get the other person to "shape up," they employ condemnation and even physical force. But the fact is that individuals who use coercive actions to try to get their partners to change are fighting a losing battle. The result is invariably that the other partner rebels, directly or indirectly, in effect responding in just the opposite way to what the first partner had hoped. Harshness will inadvertently create a result you are not seeking. Aggression begets aggression — or withdrawal.

A slow, loving, patient approach will help produce enduring change. The patient way to seek change is one of kindness, gentleness, respectfulness, courteousness. To increase intimacy, behave intimately. Demonstrate genuinely caring responses toward your partner. Go out of your way to be kind. Show respect for your partner's feelings and attitudes. Give gentle touches and hugs. Patience may come hard for you — as it does for most of us — but it will encourage your partner to reciprocate positively.

Tolerance and understanding are important aspects of patience. Intolerance shows up in both attitudes and behaviors: quickness to condemn (in your head or in your behavior) gives your partner little space for error or leeway to be an individual; interrupting or lack of flexibility in understanding your loved one's viewpoint cuts off communication and inhibits future efforts.

Couples have often forgotten how to be courteous to each other. Dr. John Gottman is an expert on couples communication who has shown that partners in conflict are able to be nice when dealing with strangers, yet — especially when dealing with touchy issues — they usually lose that ability when dealing with each other. Couples often get too familiar with each other's shortcomings, lose patience, and resort to shortcut, disrespectful communication: snapping back, profanity, or destructive teasing.

A patient, gentle, kind, respectful manner has much more persuasive power than force, coercion, or intolerance.

In short, while it may sound dull and old-fashioned, we suggest you be polite and courteous in your communication with each other regardless of the topic. By showing respect for each other, you'll get more from each other. More importantly, your intimacy will grow.

Communication Tool #2:
Verbal and Non-Verbal Listening and Speaking Skills

Remember Aaron and Robin, the couple from our workshop whom we introduced at the beginning of this chapter? The way they fought illustrates the misuse of many of the basic listening and speaking skills that are vital for good intimate communication. Take another look now at page 40 to refresh your memory of the content and process of their dialogue. Draw your own conclusions about what they did wrong. Then come back here and we'll discuss how they could have handled that situation so that both of them came out winners.

Basic listening and speaking skills (see chart on the following page) are designed to facilitate communication. Whether you are the listener or speaker the use of good *body language* will help tell your partner that you are sincere and open. Robin's glaring and Aaron's frowning would accomplish just the opposite effect.

"I" messages will also help you take responsibility for your own feelings. "I don't feel appreciated for my work efforts", is a statement that speaks for yourself rather than your partner. "You" messages are usually pronouncements or accusations:

Robin's statement, "You never do what I want" is a good example.

Basic Listening And Speaking Skills

LISTENER	SPEAKER
Use "I" messages.	Use "I" messages.
Use good body language (see "Components of Behavior" on page 50).	Use good body language (see "Components of Behavior" on page 50).
Show warmth and empathy.	Show warmth and empathy.
Use encouragers, paraphrases, summaries.	Be specific.
Ask open questions.	Stick to one topic.
Reflect feelings.	Express intentions and wants openly.
Give feedback.	Ask for feedback.

It has been estimated that more than half of human communication is by means other than *what* is said. While it's tough to tie it down precisely, *body language* — eyes, facial expression, touch and other non-verbal factors — is central to most interpersonal messages, especially in the case of intimate contact.

There must be a thousand ways we talk without words.

"Why are you looking at me that way?"

"You didn't have to say it, I saw it in your face."

"Your lips tell me no, no, but there's yes, yes in your eyes."

As we've taught assertiveness and social skills to thousands of people over the last twenty years, we've found it very helpful to identify the specific *components* of behavior which are part of every message:

Eye contact	Gestures	Fluency
Body posture	Timing	Thoughts
Distance/physical contact	Listening	Content
Voice tone, inflection, volume		
Facial expression		

We place "content" at the end of the list to emphasize that it's not as important as people often believe. Most folks bog down trying to think of "what to say" when they're trying to express themselves. Actually, we find that the other components are even more important, in most cases.

The chart on the following page summarizes the components of behavior applied to interpersonal communication.

Showing *warmth* and *empathy* can be accomplished through body language, listening skills, content, and the delivery of your message. Your partner can easily pick up on your level of positive involvement by watching these signs. It's hard to see you as warm and understanding if you're scowling, yelling, or being sarcastic! Both Robin and Aaron did some of this.

Encouragers, paraphrases, and *summaries* are listening skills which help your partner express intentions and wants openly, and also to feel understood. *Open questions* are those that can't easily be answered by a simple yes or no. "How did you answer your boss?" is a hard question to reply to with a single word response.

To *reflect feelings* means for the listener to observe the speaker's feelings carefully and to restate them openly: "Sounds like you feel angry with me." This skill also helps the speaker be aware of and clarify feelings, *be specific*, and *stick to one topic*. The process also helps both partners to know that the underlying feeling message is being heard and understood. Keep in mind that the purpose of this procedure is to deal with the *speaker's* feelings — not the response of the listener.

To improve your intimate communication, you'll find it helpful to *ask for feedback*. Asking, "What's your reaction to what I said?" can provide you with a wealth of information. *Giving feedback* in a direct and honest way helps the speaker to know the message is being received. "I feel unfairly judged about what happened; let me tell my story," is much better than Aaron's response of "Wait a minute! Hell, it doesn't happen that often." "Help" is a word that comes up a lot when we're describing these listening/speaking skills. Robin and Aaron weren't interested in helping each other solve their mutual problem. After all, isn't the basic idea of intimate communication to help each other create a better relationship? You can't do it alone!

Components Of Behavior

- *Eye Contact:* Look directly at the person to whom you are listening or speaking. (Not constantly.) Relaxed, steady attention; look away occasionally.
- *Body Posture:* Stand or sit with torso and head turned toward other, erect. Equalize height by bending, crouching, standing. Don't slouch.
- *Distance/Contact:* Arm's length is comfortable for most. Note cultural differences. Touch only if appropriate to your relationship.
- *Voice Tone, Inflection, Volume:* Conversational for most occasions. Don't shout unless you mean it. Avoid monotone, whine, sing-song. Modulate inflection and volume.
- *Gestures:* Use appropriate head, hand, and arm gestures for emphasis, warmth, openness. Strive to be uninhibited, relaxed, confident.
- *Timing:* Spontaneity of expression is desireable. Choose an occasion if the situation can't be dealt with immediately.
- *Listening:* Listen actively. Use eye contact, expression, gestures. Give feedback, Tune in, attend, understand, respond.
- *Facial Expression:* Stay consistent with content of communication (joy, firmness, anger). "Relaxed expressiveness" is the goal.
- *Fluency:* Speak smoothly. Don't rush or pause a lot. Slow down if you need time to think as you speak.
- *Thoughts:* Avoid defensiveness. Seek mutual understanding. Withhold judgement. Strive for acceptance and tolerance.
- *Content:* Honesty, openness, clarity, value. Consider your goals, and those of listener. Stay focused on key points.

Our next topic illustrates this point of mutuality in another way.

Communication Tool #3:
Breaking Intimacy-Inhibiting Communication Habits
Most folks eat too much, drink too much, stay up too late, exercise too little, communicate too poorly. Too bad. Habits which inhibit intimacy are like weeds. There are a million different varieties; they appear where they aren't wanted; they're bothersome and difficult to get rid of. But, if you truly want to, and are willing to work hard, you can overcome them. Keep a watchful eye, though. If you don't stay on top of them, all of a sudden they reappear and grow like dandelions!

Inhibiting habits also appear in the intimate landscape. Your inhibiting communication habits can be yours alone, or you can engage in them as a couple. The latter is like riding a bicycle built for two — with the riders peddling in opposite directions!

The two charts which follow help explain some common inhibiting behaviors performed by individuals and couples. Each chart includes the name of the inhibiting habit, the source, definition description, how it inhibits, and some possible solutions. As you read the charts, do two things: keep Robin and Aaron in mind, and do a little self-analysis. Identify ways *you* inhibit intimacy in your loving relationship.

Common Intimacy-Inhibiting Communication Habits
Individual

HABIT NAME	SOURCE*	DEFINITION	DESCRIPTION	WAYS IT INHIBITS	POTENTIAL SOLUTIONS
GUNNYSACKING	Bach	Collecting injustices and/or grievances which are "bottled up" or carried in a gunnysack... unspoken.	The hurts may seep out at times or all burst forth at once in a tirade.	Either it is difficult to know what he or she is thinking or when it comes out forcefully it is overwhelming.	Monitor your feelings, thoughts, reactions day by day. Try to be more constructively open and straightforward.
PSYCHO-ANALYZING	Bach; Miller, et. al.	Probing into the psychological motives of partner, character analysis and interpretation not asked for.	"You treat me this way because you have a hidden hatred for your mother."	Sidetracks the real issues. It is amateurish, patronizing, not your business.	Focus on your feelings about real issues between you. Focus on behavior and actions, not internal motivations.
LABELING, STEREOTYPING	Bach; Eisenstadt, Miller, et. al.	Placing labels on the partner's actions using incorrect generalizations.	"You're dumb." "All men are alike."	Faulty thinking. Emotionally hurtful. Shortsighted. Vague implications.	Be more positive. Be polite, courteous. Be specific.
CATCH-ALL PRONOUNCEMENTS SPEAKING FOR NO ONE	Eisenstadt; Miller, et. al.	Consigning a specific subject to a general category.	"It's just one of those things." "You're just having a bad day." "Whatever will he will be." "Anyone can do that."	Confusing. Illusive. Cuts off communication.	Give specific feeling statements, "I" messages. Explain yourself more.
MIXED MESSAGES	Miller, et. al.	Incongruent meanings within the same statement. One part is straight, the other is an added undercurrent.	"It pleases me that you take money from my wallet without asking and it doesn't upset you." "I love your clothes. You certainly have expensive taste." "Sometimes you almost make me feel wanted."	Difficult to sort out... should you feel good or bad. What is the real message?	Try to be congruent. Be more direct. What is your point?
SPEAKING FOR OTHERS	Miller, et. al.	Putting words or interpretations into your partner's mouth or mind.	"You don't know what you want." "You know you like it when I tease you."	Cuts off communication. May produce retaliation.	Think for yourself. Ask open questions. Check out feelings.
SUPERLATIVES	Miller, et. al.	Using global words.	Always. Never. Every time	Not specific. Not observant.	Be specific. Focus on concrete examples.

HABIT NAME	SOURCE*	DEFINITION	DESCRIPTION	WAY IT INHIBITS	POTENTIAL SOLUTIONS
SILENT TREATMENT COLD SHOULDER WITHDRAWING POUTING	Miller, et. al.	Letting others only suspect or indirectly know you are hurt or upset.	Silence with meaning. No eye contact. "Dagger" eye contact. Evasive response.	Is punishing. Prolongs pain. Confusing.	Re-start communication. Call a truce. Admit your feelings.
GUILTING	Lester, et. al.	Direct or indirect statements that imply the partner should feel guilty.	"You really hurt me." "You don't care about my feelings."	Stifles communication. Implies no fault on your part.	Use "I" statements. Don't guess at intentions.
MIND READING	Gottman, et. al.; Bach	Assuming you know what your partner is feeling.	"She feels that I don't understand her." "He just loves it when I tweak his nose."	You may be wrong! You end up speaking for your partner.	Put your thoughts into constructive words. Check out your perceptions.
HIDDEN AGENDAS	Gottman, et. al.	An issue is being discussed but another issue is the real one.	Talking about time she spends with her parents, but the real issue is does she care for me.	If hidden it cannot be dealt with or cleared up.	Explore your underlying motives and feelings. Get them out in the open to discuss. Get to the real issue.
RETRIBUTIONS	Alberti; Emmons	Behaving in an obviously drastic, immature manner to punish or get even.	Being "discovered" in the marital bed with a lover. Getting smashedly drunk. Openly flirting.	Undermines the total relationship. Cripples trust.	Get professional help.

*See the professional Appendix for more information.

Common Intimacy-Inhibiting Communication Habits
Couple

HABIT NAME	SOURCE*	DEFINITION	DESCRIPTION	WAY IT INHIBITS	POTENTIAL SOLUTIONS
CROSS-COMPLAINING	Gottman, et. al.	Each states a complaint in response to a complaint. "Tit for tat."	She: "You didn't pick up your clothes." He: "So, you forgot my lunch yesterday."	Causes a fight, no attempt at resolution.	Treat complaints as legitimate. Go into what you hear. Try to understand.
SUMMARIZING SELF SYNDROME	Gottman, et. al.	Each continually restating his or her own position.	He: "Blah, blah, blah." She: "Yak, yak, yak."	Causes a stalemate. Circular talking. Little attempt to understand.	Paraphrasing before replying. Check to see if you understand.
FAULT DECIDING	Lester, et. al.	Each proposes reasons that point to the other person as being the problem.	She: "We are going to be late because you didn't get gas for the car." He: "We were fine on time until you talked too long on the phone."	Blaming leads to hurt feelings and doesn't solve the problem.	Use "I" statements. Discuss the problem later.
TRYING TO ESTABLISH "THE TRUTH"	Lester, et. al.	Both propose viewpoints about what actually took place.	He: "You were upset that night, cried, and slept on the couch." She: "I did not sleep on the couch. My allergies were acting up and you were upset."	Arguing over specifics doesn't foster cooperation. Generally, the truth cannot be reconstructed anyway.	Start again with new issues. Keep independent journals. Use a tape recorder.
KITCHEN SINKING	Bach	Each brings up a series of issues. Soon everything but the kitchen sink is in the argument.	She: "You left the cat out last night." He: "The cat is fine. You're the one who is never happy." She: "Oh, you're just like your father." He: "Your mother is the real problem." She: "At least my mother is a good parent. I wish I could say that about you."	Did the cat ever get in? Couples get lost and don't address any one issue.	Good listening and speaking skills. Limit selves to one topic.

* See the professional Appendix for more information.

We've gathered this chart material from a variety of communication experts. And we even added one of our own. We don't assume that every possible bad habit is included. Use the charts to analyze your own behavior, individually and as a couple. Focus on yourself first. No finger pointing please. *Don't use these charts to start fights over who has which bad habit!*

Go ahead. We'll wait for you . . .

Tum da dum . . .

Still holding . . .

Okay. Did you discover something about yourself and your interactions with your partner? The charts should help you identify some faulty habits (and, we hope, provide some useful advice on eliminating the behaviors).

Not all communication-inhibiting habits are obvious to an outside observer, however. So far, we've only hinted at how *thoughts* are a factor in creating and maintaining intimacy-blocking communication.

Stay tuned.

Communication Tool #4:
Constructive Thoughts, Beliefs, and Expectations

Thoughts can be helpful or hurtful, enhancing your communication or hurting it. Thoughts may appear to be personal, private, and silent, and therefore have no power. Don't you believe it! Thoughts guide actions. Thoughts slip out, sometimes in subtle ways, sometimes blatantly, into words and behaviors that affect your partner and your relationship. Your thoughts are powerful determinants of who you are and how you act.

Partners who are unhappy about relationship issues tend to be supersensitive and may generate a variety of negative, undermining cognitions. ("Cognitions" is one of those job-security words psychologists like to use. It means *thoughts* .) Partners who are happy in the relationship will tend to generate a variety of positive, supportive cognitions. The box below presents examples of the inhibiting type of cognitions. (Yeah, well . . . we're psychologists, too.)

Fifteen Ways To Block Intimate Communication

1. "A good husband should be strong and assertive."
2. "A good wife should be demure and sensitive."
3. "Disagreements between partners is destructive."
4. "Men are all alike."
5. "Women are all alike."
6. "If I ask for intercourse during the week, she'll get mad."
7. "He's going to spend too much money when he goes fishing."
8. "She'll be too easy on our son when he gets a bad grade."
9. "If I mention that he's late for dinner, he'll sulk."
10. "When we go to the party, I know she'll drink too much."
11. "He's selfish."
12. "She was trying to make me mad."
13. "He was nice only because his parents were visiting us."
14. "She's nicer to our dog than she is to me."
15. "He sits in front of the TV for hours."

Where do these inhibiting thoughts come from? Psychological researchers Stephen Schlesinger and Norman Epstein suggest three sources:

Beliefs about Relationships — these usually generate from early life experiences learned from our parents, church school, mass media. They tend to be global or general rather than specific. Numbers 1 through 5 in the list fit this category.

Expectancies — these are specific expectations that come from past experiences with your partner. You're guessing the probability that she or he will respond in a certain way in specific situations. Look at items 6 - 10.

Causal Attributions — these are causes we assign to behavior of our partners. When partners negatively monitor each other's behavior, the causes they assign are rarely laudatory! The type of thinking involved is usually "all or nothing." Look at items 11 through 15.

It's important to realize that intimacy-inhibiting thoughts are generally unrealistic and/or irrational. Most often they are preconceived notions about what "should" or "will" take place. This is not to say that they can't contain seeds of truth. Recurrent inhibiting thoughts are signals that need to be dealt with in yourself or with your partner.

Cleaning Cognitive Cobwebs: There are many ways to minimize inhibiting thoughts. We've found these four to be particularly helpful:

• *Get thoughts out in the open.* Start keeping a journal of your inhibiting thoughts. It may be difficult at first to bring them into full awareness, but you'll soon catch on. Listen intently to your "inner dialogue" and write down the negative input.

• *Understand the source and motivation behind your thoughts.* Look into your own past behavior (before you met your partner) and into the history of your relationship together. There should be much food for thought! Don't drive yourself crazy trying to get to exact causes. Just try to get the general idea of why.

• *Re-work thoughts and get more realistic.* Admit to yourself that faulty cognitions are counterproductive. Challenge the need for them. Work at not allowing such thoughts to come into your thought process. Argue with the inhibiting thoughts on rational, logical grounds. If necessary, ask your spouse for help in resolving the issues that feed your negative thoughts.

• *Generate more positive, enhancing thoughts.* As you begin to gain control over your negative thoughts, replace them with positive ones. It will take some practice, but you can do it.

Use the examples of enhancing cognitions in the box below to guide you.

Fifteen Thoughts That Enhance Intimate Communication

1. "Her good points outweigh her bad points."
2. "He's nice."
3. "I love the way she smiles."
4. "He looks so handsome standing there."
5. "I'll try harder."
6. "We can work this out."
7. "We've got a lot of good things going for us."
8. "He's just feeling moody today. It will be o.k."
9. "I know she's having a hard day and is tired."
10. "We'll get through this; it will pass."
11. "We're building a good future together."
12. "I appreciate all the good things he does for me."
13. "She does so much to help me out."
14. "He's sincere."
15. "She's very loving."

Communication Tool #5:
Learn Problem Solving Skills

The "problems" we're talking about here refer to areas of your life together that aren't going right — sore points between you. These problems often have a negative emotional history to them and may involve repeated, unsuccessful attempts at resolution. However, any old problem will do. The range can be from who takes out the trash to one's bad temper to one's difficulty with non-traditional sex (whatever that is). Various words might be used to describe problems: gripes, resentments, complaints, disputes, grievances. You'll find the following steps helpful in your effort to deal with these issues in your relationship:

• *Adopt an open, positive attitude.* Believe that you two can work together to produce change. Remove any chips from your shoulder. Try to start afresh. Be optimistic and positive. Try to view the problem as a mutual one. Try to really understand what effect the problem has on each other.

• *Identify and list problems.* Generate problem lists independently first. Share them and combine your lists into a single list, roughly in order from the problems which are easiest to solve to those which are hardest.

• *Take one problem at a time, starting with the easiest, and develop it into a short, specific statement.* Start small in order to develop a workable process. Work together and narrow down, get to the essence of the problem. What is it that bothers you, specifically? Exactly when does it take place? Can you give me an example? Talk to yourself and each other if this step starts getting a little too intense. Hang in there, be calm, remember your purpose.

• *Brainstorm at least five possible solutions to the problem.* Loosen up those brain cells! Have a little fun! This doesn't have to be a heavy process. Be creative. The more ways you can think up to handle the problem, the easier it is to find a good, workable, equally acceptable solution.

• *Identify obstacles which prevent the proposed solutions.* Would a particular solution cost a great deal of money? Is enough time available to implement the solution? Is one partner unwilling to try the solution? Would the solution cause an unbalance in the relationship or other problems?

• *Identify and work to eliminate any "payoffs" or obstacles which maintain the status quo.* It's likely that both of you are gaining some rewards for keeping things the way they are (e.g. allowing the problem to go unresolved). It's very important that you figure out those payoffs, because they'll make it difficult to change. It doesn't matter if your list is longer than your partner's, or vice versa. As you examine these lists of payoffs, you may find it necessary to look for alternative sources of reinforcement in your lives. Please do, so you can let go of the forces which may be maintaining a problem.

• *Make a decision about the best alternative to follow.* Select the best solution, one that will be acceptable to both of you, and which has a reasonable chance of success (i.e. few obstacles, easy to implement). Yes, you may need to compromise, move to the middle, give in a bit. Remember your overall relationship is much more important than getting your own way on any one issue.

• *Try out the solution and monitor the results.* Implement your joint decision. Try it out for a brief specified period of time. Then regroup and see if it's working. Some couples even set up a written contract with rewards if each meets the goal. Regular reassessment is a vital step in helping you to know if your new approach is really working. It's especially useful to keep track of specifics: use the short statements you listed in step 3 to help you *count* problem behaviors and problem-*solving* behaviors before, during, and after your attempted solution.

Communication Tool #6:
Conflict Resolution Tools
Don't be afraid to argue.

Conflict is absolutely normal—indeed, *essential*—in human relationships. It need not be destructive, and it certainly should not be violent, but it ought not be feared or avoided.

Human beings inevitably disagree. Their "territorial

boundaries" are often in dispute. They see the world — and each other — through different eyes. Take Dick and Jane:

"We were on our way home from a dinner party at the Stanford's and Dick was telling me how much he had enjoyed talking with Lorraine," Jane began, her voice hesitating a bit as her volume increased. "He suggested that I should try harder to keep up with the news, read more books... *'Be more like Lorraine* is what you mean!' I guess I shouted at him."

Dick jumped on her opening: "You *guess?* You *guess?* I'll say you shouted!" (He began to shout.) "All I did was make a suggestion as to how you could improve yourself..."

"*Improve* myself?" Jane cut him off. "I'll tell you what would improve *me:* a little help from *you!*"

And on it went...

Isn't it conflict which destroys relationships? No — it's the way we *handle* conflict which destroys relationships. Obviously Dick and Jane could brawl over their disagreement, or stew silently, or chip away at each other, or take "passive-aggressive" action (such as Jane avoiding sex or Dick deriding Jane in front of others). None of these methods of "dealing with" the issue would be constructive. Indeed, none of them *does* deal with the issue.

And that's exactly what Dick and Jane must do — *deal with the issue.* Here are a few tips from conflict-resolution experts:

Conflict is more easily resolved when both parties...

... act honestly and directly toward one another. ...are willing to face the problem openly, rather than avoiding or hiding from it.

... avoid personal attacks; stick to the issues. ...emphasize points of agreement as a foundation for discussion of points of argument.

... employ a "rephrasing" style of communication, to be sure you understand each other. ("Let me see if I understand you correctly. Do you mean...?")

. . . accept responsibility for their own feelings ("I am angry!" not "You made me mad!").

. . . avoid a "win-lose" position. The attitude that "I am going to win, and you are going to lose" will more likely result in *both* losing. By remaining flexible, both can win — at least in part.

. . . gain the same information about the situation. Because perceptions so often differ, it is good to make everything explicit

. . . develop goals which are basically compatible. If we both want to preserve the relationship more than to win, we have a better chance!

. . . clarify their actual needs in the situation. I probably don't need to *win*. I do need to gain some specific outcome (behavior change by you, more money), and to retain my self- respect.

. . . seek solutions rather than deciding who is to blame.

. . . agree upon some means of negotiation or exchange. I probably would agree to give on some points if you would give on some!

. . . negotiate toward a mutually acceptable compromise, or simply agree to disagree.

When conflict involves strong angry feelings, many people fear bringing those feelings into the open, perhaps because they have been told since early childhood that anger is bad. Recognizing the value of anger, allowing that natural feeling to be expressed nondestructively, and working toward resolution of the problem will create the conditions necessary for constructive conflict resolution, and healthy, growing relationships.

"What We Have Here Is A Failure To Communicate"

It is something of a cliche' to observe that "communication" is a central force in determining the quality of relationships. The popularity of the idea, however, makes it no less true. But to say it is not enough to solve a communication problem in your intimate organism. To do that requires time, effort, and the six key communication tools we've described in this chapter.

If you do nothing else with this book, do yourself this favor: Re-read this chapter. Try as many of the exercises and suggestions as you can. And persuade your partner to join you in developing the strongest and most effective intimate communications system the two of you can put together.

It's a lifelong project, of course, because both partners — and the intimate relationship — are growing and changing all the time. Stay with it; the payoffs are great for good communication. Indeed, marital therapists Charlotte and Howard Clinebell deem it, "the source of all types of true intimacy."

 *five*

commitment

*"Our deepest relationships are held together
by an invisible cord called commitment."*
— Lewis B. Smedes

Thought much about that "invisible cord"?

Commitment is kind of an old-fashioned notion which has come 'round again. For a couple of decades in the United States, we acted as if commitment didn't matter — or even as if it were to be avoided. Couples lived together not *until* but *instead of* getting married, as a way of showing the world that they were "liberated" individuals who were satisfied to be together "one day at a time."

Things have changed. A recent study conducted by the National Opinion Research Council at the University of Chicago gives an indication of how popular commitment has become in the last few years. A national sample of 1400 adults was asked questions about their sexual behavior. *Only about one and a half percent of married men and women said they had sex partners other than their spouses.* There are lots of reasons for that statistic, of course, not the least of which may be AIDS and other sexually-transmitted diseases. Nevertheless, those of us who believe in committed relationships can be encouraged to know that marital fidelity is almost as pure as Ivory soap!

Sexual faithfulness is only one form of commitment, however.

A broader view of commitment includes your determination to hold the relationship together, how highly you value it, and how hard you'll work to maintain it. Genuine commitment is based on caring for the other person, and valuing the relationship enough to make some personal sacrifices to ensure its success. Without commitment, a relationship cannot last — even if every other dimension is strong.

How much does your intimate relationship really mean to you?

Pat and Stan had been married only eighteen months when they realized that something was wrong. Their marriage was not turning out as either of them had expected. Their hectic job pace had allowed them very little time to nurture their relationship. They continued to enjoy some of the social and recreational group activities which had helped bring them together, but they had almost no time to themselves. They felt no closer now than when they had married. Fortunately, friends offered them their mountain cabin for a week during their second summer together. They accepted, then barely managed to get away. The escape from daily pressures gave them a wonderful chance to focus on their partnership. They stayed up late, talking for hours, filling in gaps left from their whirlwind courtship. They found more to love about each other. They revealed unspoken concerns about one another, and fears each had about their future together. They built many strong bonds by uncovering "unknowns" in their feelings toward each other. The week brought them so much closer that they vowed to give themselves a similar retreat at least once a year. Their commitment was renewed.

Commitment Is . . .

Psychotherapists John and Kris Amodeo differentiate between two types of commitment: *formal* and *process*. Formal commitments are those we make when we take vows, make promises, sign contracts, pledge ourselves. Process commitments are made day-by-day, renewed constantly, offered because we are continually rededicating ourselves to this relationship.

The Amodeos describe a sequence of commitment factors, beginning with commitment to yourself and your own highest self-development, gradually opening yourself to another person in total honesty, and finally reaching a very deep level of relating to each other — precisely *because* you've come together in total honesty. (Whew!) This idea places a lot of emphasis on "being" — as if somehow it'll all happen if you just "let it."

Sounds really nice, but in the real world it almost never works like that. People who have jobs, raise kids, ride the subway, drive the freeway, do dishes, watch TV, and fall asleep exhausted, have to work at their commitments. For most of us at least, commitments require effort, dedication, sacrifice.

Commitment almost always means that you'll pay a price. You'll sacrifice some of yourself. In fact, you may not be able to achieve all your personal goals if you're committed to another person. But you'll achieve other goals which you couldn't manage alone.

Annie and Zeke weren't much into sacrifice. In their fifteenth married year, they decided at last to seek marriage counseling. Both partners had long lists of outside interests: Annie's centered on wildlife preservation and photography; Zeke's on camping, fishing and backpacking. Both gained more pleasure from those activities than from each other. They'd been spending less and less time together, and fighting more when they did.

They had no children, felt little identity as a couple, and considered marriage counseling, as Zeke put it, "One step ahead of the divorce lawyers."

Annie and Zeke acknowledged to the counselor — and to themselves for the first time — just how weak their "invisible cord" had become. As they examined their individual and couple goals, they recalled some of the attraction factors which had drawn them together in the first place, including their common interests in outdoor activities. The counselor helped them enroll in a "couple's communication weekend." Although they were very anxious about going, they found themselves talking intimately with one another for the first time in years. They admitted that their outside "me" interests left little time or energy for their "we" interests.

After the weekend, they asked the counselor's help in figuring out how they could include a few mutual activities in their schedules. They also began to take time to talk together about themselves and their relationship — not everyday, but once or twice a week when they found a few moments. They gave the time reluctantly at first, but discovered their renewed commitment to the relationship had both of them feeling more like they had when they first married. (An unexpected improvement in their sex life helped make the "sacrifice" easier to take!)

A relationship requires nurturance, time, energy and loyalty if it is to survive. Both partners must continue to pay attention to the six dimensions of the intimate organism. If one partner insists upon being able to do anything he or she wants at any time, without regard for the other partner, it's unlikely that their partnership will last or thrive.

Theologian Lewis Smedes puts it this way: "Commitment means we surrender our freedom, individuality, and control to the relationship."

Popular author-teacher Hugh Prather agrees: "Individual growth can't take precedence over relationships . . . it ceases to be growth in the attempt."

Although in this discussion we'll tend to treat commitment as a single item, for the record we'd like to observe that "commitment" comes in several shapes and sizes.

Time commitment for example: How much of your 168-hour week do you devote to your partner and to nurturing your intimate organism?

Sexual fidelity is another obvious facet of commitment. Although the idea of fidelity was considered old fashioned for a while during the "sexual revolution" (does anybody remember the sexual revolution?), as the turn of the century approaches, most folks consider fidelity an important measure of commitment to their primary intimate partnership.

Commitment to specific actions is an important day-to-day demonstration of devotion to your intimate organism. Do you hold up your end of the bargain: chores, financial responsibility, child management, follow-through on agreements?

Long-term commitment is demonstrated by willingness to accept or overlook your partner's shortcomings, by establishing and pursuing goals together, and by letting the world know that *this* person is your "main squeeze" — today, tomorrow, next year, and into the next century.

Commitment is an active, changing process which is born in and grows out of ongoing engagement with your partner. Commitment requires partners to confront each other at times, understanding that there will be rough times and negative forces to deal with, along with the joys and achievements of a loving partnership. Part of commitment is acceptance of conditions that will not change. Not blindly, not self-destructively, not of intolerable behavior, but acceptance of each other's habits and human faults which may be disagreeable but aren't really hurting anybody.

Higher levels of commitment and devotion come from sharing joys and working out concerns together over time, including — inevitably — some uncomfortable realities.

Acceptance is the beginning of true love and the ending of ego. It is the foundation of true intimacy.

Commitments in Conflict

"Commitment" sounds like a high-level virtue, doesn't it? But what happens when your commitments to the people and institutions and beliefs in your life aren't compatible? Let's face it, your intimate partnership isn't the only object of your loyalties. What about your career? Your parents? Your children? Your friends? Your religion? Groups you belong to? Yourself?

There will always be competition for your time and your energy. It can be tough to choose whether you'll go to church with your family or to a ball game with friends. Who hasn't agonized over whose in-laws to visit at Thanksgiving? What do you do when you and your partner have theater tickets and your boss says you must stay late and help her get a report ready for tomorrow's board meeting? How about when you and your partner are deep in intimate conversation and are interrupted by an "urgent" phone call from a "friend in need"?

Perhaps you'll find the exercise "Putting Your Behavior Where Your Commitments Are" helpful in setting your own priorities when your commitments are in conflict. We hope you'll try it.

Commitment Through the Stages of a Relationship

Commitment, like the other dimensions of an intimate relationship, changes over time. By and large, it increases as the relationship grows. And the features which enhance commitment change as well. What's important at the beginning stage may diminish as you get to know each other and come to love other qualities. It is possible to generalize a bit about these stages:

Early Stage. It's a pretty rare relationship which starts out with much commitment — at least in the sense we're using that

PuttingYour Behavior
Where Your Commitments Are

The next time you find yourself torn between a commitment to your intimate partner and another demand (or temptation), ask yourself these questions:

• How much *time* have I given to my partner and/or our intimate organism this week? (Remember there are 168 hours in a week, and most folks spend about 45 at work, 50+ sleeping, 20+ eating/preparing/cleaning up, 10+ commuting, . . .)

• How much of myself do I give to each of the following activities *when I'm involved in it* (I *could* give 100% to each):

  job . . .
  playing with my children . . .
  home maintenance. . .
  disciplining my children . . .
  favorite hobby . . .
  cooking . . .
  housecleaning . . .
  reading for pleasure . . .
  listening to radio . . .
  watching TV . . .
  talking with my partner about: events of the day . . .
      the world situation . . .
      our relationship . . .
  helping a friend/family member/neighbor . . .

• How would I rank the list above according to my personal priorities: which activities have first call on my loyalties?

• Finally, as I look over my answers to these questions, how does my intimate parnership make out? Is my actual behavior consistent with what I claim is most important in my life? Do I need to make some adjustments to bring my investment of myself into line with my professed values? Is the present situation a chance to start that process?

term here. You and your partner probably came together, in your first contacts, really tentative about each other. Only after you spent a good deal of time together did you begin to think about committing to a "permanent" relationship. And, as our friend Mark said recently, "These days, who knows how 'permanent' is 'permanent' anyway?"

Some time goes by. You spend more of it together. You get to know each other, and decide this is a pretty comfortable pairing. You think about living together, or marriage, or even kids. "Whoa! That's a real *commitment!*" you realize suddenly.

Yes, it is. In fact, commitment is what makes it a permanent relationship.

Middle Stage. So you've done it.

You're committed to a long-term relationship, and it's been pretty rocky. Up and down, side to side, you've bounced along this path of partnership. You've experienced some real highs, and a few miserable lows as your relationship has grown and prospered — or withered.

Your relationship is in middle age, but your commitment is just now entering full-blown adolescence. And it's just as tumultuous as those frantic teen years. You're sure you want to be together forever — until your next giant fight when you become equally sure the relationship is doomed. You make a public show of your loyalty and devotion, while you privately plot how you're going to get more time for yourself.

Larry and Lisa did everything together. Almost all their leisure interests were shared, and they were very open with each other. They argued at times, of course, but both were committed to making their marriage succeed. After seven years, they discovered — while Larry was on a business trip — that they both enjoyed the opportunity for some time apart. Lisa sent the children to her mother's, invited some women friends from college for brunch, and had more fun than she could remember. At his business conference at a remote mountaintop retreat,

Larry had time for some valuable quiet contemplation alone. Both of them were surprised and a bit anxious about the discovery that they could enjoy themselves apart from each other. They asked for our help. Did this mean they were losing their commitment? That they didn't "need" each other any more? No, we reassured them. In fact your commitment can be strengthened by knowing that your solid relationship enables both of you to grow and to become more fulfilled as individuals. Genuine intimacy enhances the partners as much as the partnership!

Late Stage. When at last your relationship has survived its adolescent crises, you're ready to settle down and enjoy the fruits of your efforts.

Don't.

Commitment is a lifetime proposition. It demands continuous renewal. You need it as much at 70 as you do at 17. Your relationship is as vulnerable at twenty years as it is at twenty months. Theologian Lewis Smedes: "Making it last is only a way of giving people a chance to make it good."

How Commitment Relates to the Other Dimensions

Each of the systems in our *ACCEPT* model of relationships contributes to commitment. (Indeed, all six are interdependent and mutually supportive — drawing strength from each other just like an intimate couple.)

Attraction contributes to commitment by making it easier. When you and your partner are attractive to each other, you have a powerful incentive to remain a couple. The inclination many folks have to "stray" from the marriage relationship — and thus weaken if not break their commitment — is diminished when they find their partners stimulating, attractive, desirable

Not only are partners less inclined to look elsewhere when their mates are attractive, but they're more strongly reinforced for their loyalty. An attractive partner, toward who one feels drawn (by whatever definition one has for "attractive"), and in whom one can take pride for possessing those qualities, makes life more rewarding.

Herrold and Maud, for instance, were not your average married couple. They'd been together ten years when we met them, and our first impression was that this was a relationship in big trouble. Herrold was an overweight, non-communicative, forty-two year old computer consultant who worked from six a.m. to eight or nine p.m. most days. When he wasn't working on new programs or debugging somebody's botched do-it-your-self project, he was evaluating and bidding on new jobs to keep his fledgling company afloat. Maud, meanwhile, was a fiery, beautiful twenty-nine year old dancer who could have her way on most any stage in this hemisphere. How they got together is a story unto itself. The attraction that *held* them together was simple: *they brought out the best in each other, and they genuinely enjoyed being together* — when they *were* together. In their case, attraction was not the issue (though it looked that way to the casual observer). Their problem was that Herrold had a tiger by the tail (his growing business) and Maud wanted more from life than the promise that "things will be better when . . ."

Communication is another key element in commitment, of course. The feeling of mutual trust, which builds from openness and honesty with one another, leads to strong bonds. Willingness to share one's inmost thoughts and feelings — when they are of concern to the partner — is a powerful statement of commitment, and a builder of commitment.

Jonie and Gerry didn't find that very easy, however. Jonie was a school teacher — a college grad who was working on a master's degree and credential to teach in the community college. Gerry had completed his high school work in a continuation school while working on his dad's cattle ranch. She was talkative and open; he kept pretty much to himself. They had dated in early high school years, then got together again when Jonie came back after college to teach in the same school.

Their attraction to each other had been mostly physical at first, but had grown as they shared mutual interests in animals, living in the country, building a home, and volunteering at their church. Married three years, they had begun to drift apart because their communication seemed to have floundered on the barrier of her openness vs. his reticence.

Enjoyment makes "sticking together" less "sticking" and more "together." Couples who *play* together tend to *stay* together. If your relationship is filled with enjoyment, commitment is going to be *fun*.

Matt and Jolene are a great example of this. Fun was their life. They loved to participate actively in sports, belonged to a tennis club, and sailed their small boat regularly. Yet they rarely took part in the highly competitive tournaments and meets sponsored by their tennis and sailing friends. They were doing what *they* genuinely enjoyed, and thought these activities were good healthy ones for their children as well.

Dyane and Eldon had fun in very different ways. They were less athletic than Matt and Jolene, more oriented to "indoor sports." Their favorite activities centered on handwork hobbies — Dyane worked with ceramics, and Eldon with model cars and trains — and a regular Thursday night bridge game with a group which had been meeting on and off for fifteen years. Some folks thought their lives rather "dull," but they knew they were doing exactly what brought *them* pleasure.

And pleasure, even more than beauty, really is in the eye of the beholder!

Purpose — as the central core of an intimate organism — is the "catalyst" for your commitment glue. Without it, the bond is not just weaker, it simply doesn't exist. Without clear purpose, a relationship may maintain for many years, but it will never develop a strong sense of "we-ness," of identity as a partnership.

Jimmy and Rosalyn Carter are good examples of a purposeful, committed relationship. Although the former President and Governor held those offices alone, Mrs. Carter was one of the most involved and active First Ladies in memory. Her input into his policy decisions, in fact, was resented by many politicians. After leaving the White House, the Carters have remained active in public affairs as a team — including side-by-side work for the low-income housing program "Habitat for Humanity."

Trust and commitment are inevitably linked. Fred and Wilma hang in together for lots of reasons, but even the strongest underpinnings of their commitment would be strained severely by a significant breakdown of trust. And once broken, it's *really* tough to rebuild trust. (Tough, but not impossible, as we'll discuss in Chapter Eight.)

Dozens — perhaps hundreds — of country-western songs are centered on the theme of broken trust. Some suggest that "trust" means it's okay as long as I can "trust" that you'll come home to me eventually — that your "indiscretion" didn't really "mean anything." You were just far from home and lonesome. Others give the idea that a breakup over violated trust is to be regretted — I wish I hadn't sent you packing just because you strayed. Acceptance is indeed the core value of committed relationships, but Fred and Wilma will probably be better off if they agree on some limits — then trust each other within those boundaries.

"Will you still love me, when I'm sixty-four?" Can I trust you to be there for me when I need you — tomorrow, next year, "when I'm old and grey"?

The Trouble With Commitment

Commitment is a positive value in healthy relationships, but it's not an absolute.

Blind commitment — the "press on regardless" school of relationships — is a source of much misery in the world. Ann Landers and her sister Abigail Van Buren regularly receive letters from adults whose parents "stayed together for the sake of the children." The *children's* view — almost invariably — is that everyone in the family would have been better off if the parents had long since parted. The children might have benefitted from an opportunity to see healthier — and honest — models of parenting, and the parents might have had a chance at happiness themselves.

Getting puffed-up with one's own righteousness is another hazard which may accompany "commitment." Couples who celebrate a silver (25th) wedding anniversary are often heard to remark about how few others reach that milestone. They may be right, but does that make them better people than their friends and neighbors who broke up earlier? We think not.

Consider the range of possibilities for sticking it out vs. ending a marriage.

In previous generations, and in some social, cultural, and religious groups yet today, marriage was considered literally "till death do you part." No divorce was recognized, no reason to dissolve the union considered valid. Marriage to a divorced person was forbidden, because that person was looked upon as already married.

At the opposite extreme, another sizeable segment of society saw *any* reason one partner wanted out of a marriage as okay. Dissatisfied with your sex life? Find another partner. No interests in common? There's bound to be somebody out there who shares your world view. Spouse holding back your "fulfillment"? Hit the road, Jack.

For most of us, however, good judgement suggests a middle ground. There are circumstances which justify dissolving a committed relationship. But they are certainly not as common as the advocates of marital freedom would have us believe. Nor are they as rare as the hard-line forces of "forever" insist.

Exactly where to draw the line which says "okay" on this side and "no" on that side? We can't draw that line for you — but we'd probably suggest you take a few giant steps back from where you're standing . . .

Jack Barranger, in his book *Knowing When to Quit*, advises that we *can* know ourselves well enough to recognize when it's time to end a commitment. Barranger offers a "Knowing When to Quit Index," as a way of scoring one's feelings about a dead-end relationship. If you're having any serious thoughts about breaking your own intimate ties, we encourage you to get hold of a copy of Jack's book and complete his questionnaire. You may surprise yourself.

Building Commitment

Here are some practical ideas for building a more committed relationship. Add these to your homework for this chapter, and go to work renewing your commitment right now.

- Don't make promises you can't keep.
- Don't make promises you won't keep.
- Be faithful in small things.
- Repledge yourselves to each other *aloud* occasionally.
- Keep short-term "distancing" (arguments) in perspective, realizing they are inevitable and will pass if not blown out of proportion.
- Read the "Purpose" chapter and keep working to make the purpose of your relationship clear, agreed upon, achievable, valuable, . . .
- Keep a journal, and read about the good times when things get tough.
- Watch for the patterns in your relationship. Most hassles are cyclical, and often triggered by similar events. You may be able to break the pattern, but if not, at least by recognizing it you'll keep it in proper perspective and not assume the worst every time!
- Examine the other five key dimensions of your relationship — attraction, communication, enjoyment, purpose, trust — and look for ways each can be strengthened to help build your commitment.

Popular writer Judith Viorst is pretty unequivocal about commitment: "Married life. Is it worth it? Yes, it's worth it. Yes, it is. It's worth it because the man in my bed is the man I still want to be there. It's worth it because that man still makes me feel loved."

six

enjoyment

"Are We Having Fun Yet?"

Having fun, enjoying life and each other, making the most of each day, taking an active part in recreational and leisure pursuits — these are the nourishment all of us need to carry us through. A vital intimate organism gives enjoyment to each partner, and contributes its vitality to the larger community.

"True intimacy is when two people delight each other and delight in each other," says psychology professor Peter Kalellis. We especially like the word *delight*. It brings to mind pictures of two-year-olds splashing in the bathtub, ten-year-olds riding off-road bikes over the mounds in a vacant lot (are there still any vacant lots?), college students walking hand-in-hand, grandparents bringing Christmas gifts . . .

Yes, this is a serious discussion of intimacy, but let's not overlook the importance of fun. Intimate partners need to *enjoy* their life together. Even if the couple is "holding on" out of (social, physical, or economic) necessity, each partner needs some pleasant experiences to make it all worthwhile.

Enjoyment, of course, is unique to each individual. You may find it "fun" to stand on a windy beach on an icy day, looking forward to a romp in the near-freezing surf, as do "Polar Bear" groups in the U.S.A. and the U.S.S.R. Other folks enjoy hours in dark, noisy halls, laying money on green tables in hopes that cards (or dice or wheels) will smile on them. One man seems as happy polishing his sports car as another is caressing his lover. Some women love to be creative in a loft studio, others get their joy from creating deals in the boardroom.

"But I'm an adult now. I've got to act grown up, not play silly kids' games."

No argument, most of the time. But does that mean you must never "fool around," never enjoy yourself, never play games? We sure hope not! Accepting yourself includes nurturing the child in you.

Actor Richard Dreyfuss puts it beautifully: "Retain the childlike and discard the childish."

It's Easy to Make Yourself Miserable

Isn't fun what it's all about?

"Maybe for some people," say you, "but I've got *responsibilities* — serious matters to think about."

We believe you, and so have we. We're not suggesting that you (or we) neglect the serious demands of survival and security and success. But at the very least, don't make yourself *unhappy*. Try to avoid attitudes like this one, captured by popular writer and humorist Judith Viorst in a brief excerpt from a "letter to relatives":

"*Hi Everybody*,"

"*We're all fine. The chest pains only bother me at bedtime and if I don't move my shoulder I hardly notice the arthritis . . .*"

Psychologist Paul Watzlawick, in his very entertaining and instructive book, *The Situation is Hopeless, but not Serious*, describes dozens of ways we can make our lives miserable. With tongue in cheek, brain in gear, and pen in hand, Dr. Watzlawick offers a virtual "cookbook" of recipes to make yourself *unhappy*. Here's a sample:

"The mere fact that other people may recommend something becomes the very reason for rejecting it . . ."

Watzlawick identifies "four games with the past" which some folks play to add to their misery:

Glorification of the past, in which everything which happened long ago looks better than anything happening now;

Mrs. Lot, who failed to see the possibilities in the present and future;

The Fatal Glass of Beer, which recalls W.C. Fields' film of that name as an example of how we blame fate or a "critical event" in the past for our unhappiness today; and

The Lost Key, in which he recounts the old tale of the man who, having lost his keys in the dark, looks for them under a street lamp because "it's too dark over there where I lost them."

There are more in Watzlawick's fine essay, including *Chasing Away the Elephants* ("But there are no elephants around here." "See, it's working!"), and *If You Really Loved Me, You Would Like Garlic*. His point is simple, yet as complex as human nature itself: We hold on to hundreds of false ideas which get in the way of enjoying our daily experience. Beating ourselves (and our partners) over the head with these ideas, is definitely not healthy for our intimate organisms.

Here are a few more ways folks squash enjoyment in intimate relationships:

* *Power struggles* ("Who's in charge here, anyway?")
* *Issues of control* (Over money, children, time, space)
* *Workaholism* ("Just let me finish this . . .")
* *Values which downplay pleasure* ("Nice people don't . . .")
* *Economic circumstances* ("We can't afford it")

- *Habituation* (The more you do it, the less fun it is.)

The solution to all of this? Simple: You made your bed of misery, now throw the covers on the floor and start over to make yourself a happy sleeper! The rest of this chapter has ideas which can help.

Humor Your Senses

Stand-up comics, improvisational comedy, slapstick movies . . . humor is back in style. Even 1960s style. TV's strongest bid for humor-amidst-agony during those difficult years — Rowan and Martin's *Laugh-In* — made a comeback of sorts in the 1980's: re-runs of the popular NBC-TV laugh-at-the-news-so-you-won't-cry commentary found an audience on a popular cable network two decades later.

Laughing at professional entertainers, however, has its limitations. Who can compete at home with the teams of writers behind *Cosby* or *Cheers* or *Roseanne*? How do ordinary couples maintain the chuckles after they turn off Johnny Carson or Arsenio Hall?

Developing your own sense of humor doesn't require a script, of course, but it does demand some effort. An important first step is *careful observation* of what's going on around you. The wheezes of your aging car, the antics of your cat, the way your three-year-old can get your goat, the latest shenanigans in Washington or city hall — all are grist for your humor mill. What's more, you and your partner are probably pretty funny yourselves, if you take a step back and really look at your daily activities. How do you work out the arrangements for who showers first, who feeds the dog, who stops at the grocery on the way home, who unwinds the three-year-old at bedtime?

Humor Log

Use a log/diary/journal to take some notes for a day. Jot down six or more situations you came across today which could have a funny side. Don't overlook any possibilities: taking out the trash (did the bag break?); finding a parking place at work or shopping; people you see in a store; your dog's response when you entered the yard; a traffic jam; the boss's attempt at a joke; a bear you saw while on vacation; a strange phone call. For each item, make some notes which will help you to recall your own reactions, what was said, whether anyone laughed at the time. Would you laugh if it happened to someone else?

If you *depersonalize* your life activities, taking them out of the context of "you and your partner," aren't some of them really pretty amusing? What about the other day when you had to get out of the shower to find the shampoo? And when you went back into the house three times before you could leave to go shopping for a couple of hours: You forgot your sunglasses, the clothes that had to go to the cleaners, and the bills you were going to mail. Then you got downtown and drove around for 20 minutes looking for a parking place. Did you fume, or make fun?

Now think about how Bill Cosby or Eddie Murphy or David Letterman might describe such foibles. *You can turn minor trouble into a joke* — just the way you've seen comics do it on TV, from *I Love Lucy* to *M*A*S*H* to *Night Court.*

Comedy Scripts

Pick three of the situations you noted in Exercise A above, and write a short story describing each in the words of your favorite comedian. If you have trouble with this, just picture the episode as a vignette on *The Cosby Show* and write the dialogue.

Laugh at yourself. It's not really you — it's the human condition we all share which is funny. Look for and find ways to let yourself lighten up and enjoy it.

Keep building your capacity to smile when things go awry. Remind yourself — changing your thoughts as we discussed in Chapter 5 — that things *will* go wrong and you need to expect it, be prepared for it, find a way out of it, and enjoy the process.

Laughing At Yourself

Next time you do something you think is foolish, or make a mistake at a simple task (reach for a door handle and miss, spill a cup of coffee, grind the gears on your car), tell yourself "That would be really funny if I saw someone else do it on *Candid Camera* or *America's Funniest Home Videos.*" Then have a good laugh at yourself — instead of kicking yourself around the block!

Humor is always more fun when it's shared. Approach life's humorous situations — and the process of developing your own sense of humor — as a *team* sport. You and your partner will have more than twice the fun you'd have alone!

More Joy in Your Sex Life

Sex, as we've observed before in this book, is often thought of as a synonym for intimacy. If the TV news commentator says, "They were reported to have had an intimate relationship," the implication is that "they" were *sexually* intimate. As you've seen, sex is only one part of the intimate organism — but that doesn't mean it's not important.

The sexual relationship is arguably the most evident quality of an intimate partnership, in part *because* it is such a central theme in the popular culture and the media. When the discussion in his couples group turned to sex, Anthony pulled no punches: "Hey — sex is *important* to me. If Judy isn't interested when I am, we've got trouble."

Sometimes, however, "Judy" isn't interested because when "Anthony" says "sex" he means the same routine, "wham-bam-thank-you-ma'm" approach to intercourse which has characterized their physical relationship for the past four years. "Is that all there is to sex?" is Judy's lament.

There may not be a Santa Claus, Judy, but there is more to sex than what you and Anthony have discovered so far. Here are just a few ideas for increasing your enjoyment of physical intimacy:

- *Get spontaneous.* Don't wait for "Saturday night" — or whatever your "regular" time may be — for sex.
- *Look for new and innovative places* for sex. In front of the fireplace, in the back of the station wagon, in the hammock . . .
- *Take time for sex.* Get away if that's the only way you can get time without interruptions.
- Forget the results and *enjoy the process* for a change. Give yourself up to great sensations of touch and movement before, during, after — *or instead of* — coitus.
- *Add some romance* to your sexual endeavors. Flowers, wine (not too much!), candlelight, a fire in the fireplace, sensuous music . . . Don't just march into the bedroom to "do it."
- *Talk to each other.* Find out what your partner *really* enjoys, and tell what you enjoy. Pleasure each other!
- *Forget your sensible, rational side* when sex is the subject. Let your irrational, emotional, childlike qualities take charge. Playfulness has its own rewards.
- *Read — together —* some of the better books on sex which have appeared in recent years. Pay attention to the author's credentials — but look primarily for an emphasis on fun and mutual pleasure. (Alex Comfort's *Joy of Sex* is a great place to start.)
- Don't take it so seriously! Laugh and giggle together. Joke,

tickle (don't overdo this!) — make *fun* your goal, and orgasm is likely to take care of itself.

Laugh It Up With the Joneses

Notice how your friends and neighbors have fun. Here are a few folks we've seen enjoying themselves:

A distinguished professor of architecture at our local university (which, incidentally, has one of the largest and finest schools of architecture in the country), Fred often works out elegant design solutions with his children's wooden building blocks.

Joann sticks a favorite stuffed animal in her husband's suitcase when he goes on a business trip, so he takes a "part of her" with him.

Maurice reminds his wife she's nagging him by saying — in an exaggerated little-boy way — "OK, *Mom*."

Carla and Tony have a "singles date" with each other two or three times a year to help keep their romance fresh.

Elysse rented a Corvette and "gave" it to Jeremy for a day on their anniversary — as a joke to help loosen up his penny-pinching.

Tanya runs around the house shouting and pounding on things in an intentionally exaggerated response to Raymond's "reminders" about projects she's left unfinished.

Albert turns cartwheels on the courthouse lawn as he and Jennifer walk by each evening. (They became grandparents this year.)

Suzanne begins each meeting of the Board of Directors of her publishing business with a game of "twenty questions."

Darrell meets Roxanne at the door when she comes home from work — often with a drink ready, sometimes with a funny game or riddle, occasionally nude . . .

"A little sparkle," says comedian Roy Blount, Jr., "goes a long way."

Fun Is Where You Find It — So Get Looking!

• *Do things which will please your partner.* Nearly everybody starts out love relationships making extra efforts to show their partners how special they are and how much they are loved. After a while, the novelty, excitement, and joy of those efforts start to wear thin — on both sides. Jim gets tired of looking for flowers or new restaurants or special knick-knacks. Linda finds his lack of creativity boring.

Sometimes, even if they keep up the pace, the sheer fact of repetition wears the shine off the apple. Psychologists call this process *habituation*. Dr. Neil Jacobson, marital psychologist and professor at the University of Washington, refers to "reinforcement erosion": the gradual wearing-away of positive feelings that used to come from everyday acts of love, for both giver and receiver. Do everything you can to keep your fun fresh and new. (Try a few of the "101 Ways . . ." listed later in this chapter.)

• *Seek Joy:* More than fun, more than pleasure, more than happiness, genuine *joy* is the deep inner sense of aliveness, wholeness, and spontaneous energy which — usually only for a moment or two — eclipses everything else. A baby's laugh, a beathtaking sunset, a lover's unexpected appearance can bring this wonderful feeling. Treasure it. Nurture the situations and relationships which bring it. And *share it with your partner!*

• *Inventory Your Enjoyment:* Develop a list of enjoyable activities — individually and together. What brings you pleasure? Where do you turn for fun? Do you and your partner have mutual entertainment and leisure interests? Do you take time to relax, to get away from chores and work? Keep a "fun log" and read it occasionally to help you recall — and recreate — special fun times. Don't rob your relationship of enjoyment by overwork or overemphasis on the future, or by missing opportunities to gain pleasure from current activities together — hobbies, travel, games, social life . . .

• *Cultivate Playfulness:* What are your leisure acitvities? Do you take time for nonpurposeful games and play? Do you allow the "child in you" to surface and enjoy itself? Is gentle kidding part of your partnership communication? Can you play non-competitively — just for the fun of it? Do you ever "go fly a kite"? Ride a bike (for pleasure)? Run on the beach? Make a joke in a crowded elevator? Turn a cartwheel in the street?

• *Make fun in your work.* It's been said that the difference between work and fun is who's holding the paintbrush (remember Tom Sawyer and the whitewashed fence?) Can you have fun at the doctor's office? On an airplane? Waiting in line at the bank? Fun is where you find it. You and your partner *could* be looking for it all the time!

• *Learn to relax.* Not just "feet-up-in-front-of-the- TV" relaxing. We mean intentional, all-over-your-body, deep muscle relaxation. You can buy any of several relaxation training audiotapes; or you can read and follow the relaxation instructions in any of the many good books on the subject (see Benson & Klipper in the Bibliography). You can teach yourself simply by concentrating on each of the major muscle groups in your body, one at a time, and alternately tensing and relaxing them. Tense a group of muscles for a few seconds (e.g. your hand and forearm), and pay attention to how it feels when tight. Then let go, and follow that feeling of release as the tightness flows out of your fingertips.

• *Recall activities you've enjoyed in the past.* Make a list of all the things you can think of that you have enjoyed doing in your life. Remember Christmas or Hannukah when you were a kid? How about summer vacation? Playing ball? Jumping rope? Going to the movies? How many of those activities can you re-create now? Can you and your partner do them together? If not, can each of you help and support the other in doing some of them?

• *Reconnect with old friends.* Are there some folks you haven't seen in months or years? How about you and your partner calling them on the phone tonight? Or making an audio cassette tape and sending it to them?

- *Find your music.* Did you — like most kids — try and later quit piano lessons when you were in elementary school? Do you like music, but find it frustrating that you can't play an instrument? How about a player piano? (Some new models even have computerized magnetic tape controllers!) Simple electronic keyboards can be mastered by nearly anyone. Or, you could even take piano (guitar, flute . . .) lessons now! Music is a great area for sharing as an intimate couple.

- *Identify your own strengths.* Don't be inhibited or embarrassed. Everyone has *at least* a few good qualities! After each of you completes a personal list of strengths — no criticisms, please! — exchange lists and each partner then can add to the other's list. Again, no criticisms. And no denying or contradicting your own or your partner's lists!

- *Take time out.* When did you last treat yourself to an evening at the symphony, a basketball game, a theater performance? Why not season tickets, so you'll *schedule* some time together for an evening of entertainment on a regular basis?

- *Turn stress on its head.* Make a list of the major sources of stress in your life (job, relationships, money, . . .). Discuss each stressor with your partner, and come up with two or three specific steps you can take to turn each stressor into a source of fun.

- *Play with kids.* Join a group working with youngsters: Special Olympics, Big Brothers, Scouts, the Y, community band, swim club, after-school or summer recreation, school volunteers.

- *Expand your horizons.* Here are some sources of enjoyment others have found. Do any suggest possibilities for you and your partner? Consider these: art, music, sport, relaxation, relationships, children, beauty in nature, achievements, games, humor, material goods, home environment, having money, earning money, saving money, spiritual experience, personal fulfillment, watching entertainment, animals, food, sex, intellectual stimulation, satisfying work, learning, travel, rewards, recognition, loving, being loved, dancing, vacations, massage.

• *Emphasize the positives.* Psychiatrist Aaron Beck, in his recent popular book, *Love is Never Enough*, suggests a couple of specific things partners can do to let their mates know what pleases them:

"...try to notice methodically what your mate already does that pleases you ... write down each instance ... Simply keeping track of the small pleasures of their married life makes a couple more aware of the actual degree of satisfaction ...

"Whenever your spouse does something that pleases you, it should be followed up with a reward of some kind — an appreciative note, or a kiss, for example. Rewards are a far better way than punishment to change how your spouse acts."

• *ACCEPT fun.* Look for fun in each of the six major dimensions of your intimate relationship: Attraction, Communication, Commitment, Enjoyment, Purpose, and Trust.

101 Ways to Have More Fun

An intimate partnership is a particularly fertile field for fun. Since you're sharing a great deal of time and space together, you want to maximize the pleasure you gain from the relationship. And you want to make it possible for your partner to have a lot of fun too. How to do that?

• *Get to know yourself*, so you know what you really enjoy doing.

• *Get to know your partner*, so you know what s/he really enjoys doing.

• *Look for chances to have fun spontaneously* every day (by your *attitude* as well as your *activities*).

• *Make time for planned fun.*

• *Try a new game*, sport or recreational activity at least twice a year.

• *Be a careful observer* of people — notice how others have fun, and consider trying their styles.

- *Make work into fun* by inviting others to help.
- *Volunteer.* Get involved in giving some time and energy — together — to the community, or schools, or church, or youth groups, or the homeless, or . . .
- *Surprise your partner* with an unscheduled gift or activity you think s/he would enjoy.
- *"Trade pleasures"* with each other once in a while by doing something one of you enjoys which is of little interest to the other. (You may be surprised at what *you* learn to enjoy!)
- *Make up lots of enjoyable activities* which are unique to your relationship (jokes, games, facial expressions, pet names, mini-vacations, favorite music, shows, dances, . . .).
- *Read: More Joy in Your Marriage, Playfair, Intimate Play, We Are Still Married, Love and Marriage.*
- *List things you could do* — brainstorm this alone — which your partner would enjoy or which would make her/his life more pleasant.
- *Do some of the things* you listed above. Don't *tell* your partner what you're doing. And do it because you *want* to, not for praise or some selfish motive.
- *Find a job you love* and work at it.
- *Pursue happiness.* Make it a priority in your life.

Finally, follow the advice of our psychologist friend Michael Mantell: *"Don't sweat the small stuff."* (And remember: It's *all* small stuff!)

 *seven*

purpose

"Where there is no vision, the people perish."
— **Proverbs 23:18.**

Paul and Priscilla are a classic "love at first sight" couple. They met in college, married after graduation, and have been together more-or-less happily for three years. Although they have no children now, they've talked about "when we have a family" in the future. Both are employed in well-paid career positions with large companies, and they enjoy the comfortable lifestyle their substantial incomes have afforded them. They have many friends in similar circumstances.

In recent months, Paul has begun to feel vaguely dissatisfied with the relationship. He can't pinpoint anything either he or Priscilla has done — or not done — but he thinks "things could be much better." Priscilla asks from time to time if anything's wrong, but Paul just shrugs it off.

Priscilla and Paul rarely discuss where they're headed in their life together, except that they hope to buy a home in a year or two, and to take a summer trip to Europe. They seldom see their relatives, since both families live in another state.

Here's a couple whose outward appearance of success would be envied by many, yet Priscilla and Paul aren't really happy with their lives. Their only real goal is to improve their careers and financial status. They aren't planning to build a family, or to help their original families, or to contribute to the community, or to pursue any values or aims other than economic success. Theirs is an intimate organism without goals or intent. They haven't grown beyond the initial attraction which brought them together.

Paul and Priscilla's situation isn't at all unusual. Many, many couples have given little thought to purpose in their lives together. Maybe you're among them?

Think about your own intimate union. Why did you commit yourself to your relationship in the first place? Why do you stick it out? What does the alliance give to you? To your partner? To the world?

Purpose is a motivating force, a guiding principle which can help you define your goals and objectives, for your intimate organism. Purpose, or lack of it, determines whether your intimate organism works or flounders. Purpose defines the connections among yourselves, your relationship, and your environment. Among the many realms of purpose are your views of how the world "should be" and your ideas about politics, social conditions, child rearing, spiritual experiences, human life, the environment, human relationships.

This very complex and dynamic dimension is central to the success and stability of the intimate relationship, providing a star to guide you, a rudder to steer with. Without purpose, you're likely to float at the whims of the tide, rather than making intentional progress. You may, as the prophet suggests, even "perish" as a couple. Somebody put it well: "If you don't know where you're going, you're likely to wind up somewhere else."

In this chapter, we'll be examining three aspects of purpose:

- Your *life purposes* as two individuals.
- Your *shared goals and direction* — what you hope to accomplish in your life together.
- The *strength of your commitment* to your intimate organism.

At the close of the chapter, we'll offer a few specific suggestions for building purpose in your own loving partnership.

Individual Life Purposes of Each Partner

Ultimately, each of us is alone. Despite your commitment to your partner — and your willingness to put the partner's best interests above your own for a time — you must take care of yourself. And so must your partner. If an intimate relationship is to survive, it must in some ways serve the purposes and needs of each of the partners.

Have you made *nurturing your individual needs and your partner's* one of the important purposes of your love relationship?

Individual needs may be global or personal, lofty or mundane. You or your partner may aspire to high political office or to make as much money as possible. Some folks wish to complete a graduate degree, or learn to drive a racing car. Others set their sights on working as volunteers in poverty areas or holding secure jobs in affluent neighborhoods.

Of course, your goals and purpose may change in time. Susan and Bob graduated from college with a specific goal: to make money in business for several years, then use their nest egg to relocate to a quiet rural area and develop a pre-school for young children. After they both earned MBAs, things began to change. Susan's career took off, Bob's languished. Now, ten years after college, they have two small children of their own, Bob is a full-time homemaker and "Mr. Mom," and Susan is a fast-rising corporate executive. They're not sure where they go from here (or when), but it's not going to be easy to walk away from Susan's success.

It helps, of course, if your values and goals are in agreement with those of your partner. You may harm your intimate organism by working overzealously toward individual goals which may get in the way of your relationship. Many worthwhile social programs require hours of volunteer work, and many careers in service to others require strange hours and extended work schedules. These commitments inevitably conflict with the personal needs of a partnership, and — despite the partner's patience, tolerance, and shared support — can lead to relationship problems. If you are involved in such a situation, take extra pains to nurture your intimate relationship as well as you nurture your career or volunteer efforts.

Cheryl and Ken met in college, where both were actively involved in environmental activities. Six years later, they're married and live in a small midwest town where Ken is director of the community recycling program. Cheryl supports the program, but she resents the four or five evenings and Saturday mornings every week which Ken now spends away from her and their six-month old daughter.

Whatever your personal purposes in life, mutual support for each other's individual goals and needs is an appropriate and necessary purpose of your intimate partnership. Don't neglect it. And remember that communicating about each of your individual goals and needs is a vital aspect of providing this mutual support.

Communication is also needed when your individual goals clash. You may have differences in terms of scheduling or other legitimate concerns, such as how much time one should devote to individual pursuits or how much money is needed for individual purposes. Both partners have individual purposes, and both have the total intimate organism to care for. These issues will be discussed at greater length in Chapter Nine ("Intimacy Respects Individuality").

Charting Your Individual Purposes

The "map" below offers a systematic way to examine purpose in your life. The list down the column at the left represents most of the important realms of human existence. The items across the top are the people and environments with which we live. You can easily review the breadth and depth of your own purposes by filling in each of the boxes on the chart.

As you examine your own purposes, you'll find the size of box you need will vary widely from realm to realm. In some boxes you'll make no entry; you may have no particular goals or interest in that area. (You may, for example, have no concern with the "aesthetic" realm in relation to your intimate relationship or family). In contrast, another box may overflow. (You will very likely have quite specific purposes in the "family/health & safety" box.)

The "boxes" are tiny on the book page, of course, but you can make each one as large as it needs to be to make room to write your own list of purposes.

Purpose Map

	Self	Partner-ship	Family	Others	Society	Environ-ment
Spiritual						
Psychological						
Social						
Political						
Economic						
Vocational						
Aesthetic						
Recreational						
Intellectual						
Health & Safety						
Environmental						

If you and your partner both complete the map, your responses under the heading of "Self" will likely show some areas of similarity, but also some that are unique for each person.

We suggest you use the "Purpose Map" in two ways:

• Take as much time as you can — now and in the next few days — to write down your entries for each box. You may find it helpful to use a small notebook, allowing a separate page for each box. For example, the first (upper left corner) box might read like this:

"*Spiritual Purpose — Myself:* I don't think much about spiritual purposes these days. I do believe in a Supreme Being — not "God" exactly. I think all human beings have some sort of spiritual connection. I guess my 'purpose' in this realm would be to try to find or articulate a belief system which expresses my ideas."

Each partner should complete a separate individual Purpose Map, then get together and share your personal purposes, topic by topic. Be prepared for some surprises, and be prepared to support your partner's goals in life.

• Keep your written Purpose Map, and refer to it periodically — at least twice a year. Update it when appropriate as your goals change. Make special note of major changes in the direction and purpose of your life — as individuals and as a couple. Pay particular attention to the factors that bring about such changes in your purposes. Becoming aware of the forces which are most influential in your life is a major step in knowing yourself. Sharing that insight with your partner will help shape your mutual purposes, and build trust and intimacy in your partnership.

Partnership Patterns and Purposes

Every relationship exists for a reason — or maybe a dozen reasons.

Psychiatrist Martin Blinder in his book *Choosing Lovers,* has identified eight patterns of intimate relationships, based upon the needs of the two partners involved. In his words:

". . .what makes all love relationships, from adolescent crushes to lifelong marriage, so intriguing and complex, is that they involve two peple in constant motion and flux. . . our personality structure and degree of emotional maturity make our choice of partner remarkably predictable. We do not fall in love by coincidence."

Dr. Blinder's eight relationship patterns shed much light on purpose in the intimate organism. Here's a brief summary:

• *Validating Relationships* are based on the need of one or both partners for another person to affirm his or her value as a person. Such individuals lack a solid sense of self-worth, and are seeking to bolster weak egos through a love relationship. Validating relationships are unlikely to last, but can teach both partners much about their own needs, and prepare them to move on to healthier partnerships.

• *Structure-Building Relationships* are future oriented, designed to provide for long-range goals and tasks, such as children, a home, financial security. The focus in these partnerships is on comfort, security, success in the world, rather than intimacy or the feelings of the partners. Structure-building couples are living the roles of achievers, problem solvers, good citizens, and are probably gaining in maturity along the way. Structure-building relationships can be long lasting, but may offer little emotional nourishment for the partners.

• *Experimental Relationships* provide a testing ground — a chance for individuals to spread their wings and perhaps to live out their romantic fantasies. Often sexually focused ("Many extramarital affairs," says Blinder, "are, in fact, experimental relationships"), these unions are usually short-lived and may be very intense. At their best, experimental relationships can offer learning opportunities; the key is to recognize that the partnership *is* experimental, and to learn the needed lessons and move on.

• *Avoidance Relationships* can provide needy partners a shield against vulnerability and commitment. Folks who are unable or unwilling to risk investing themselves in an emotionally demanding intimate partnership may choose distant, superficial, low-commitment avoidance relationships. These loose partnerships offer, says Blinder, "safe havens," allowing partners to remain at "arm's length" from a truly intimate committed relationship.

• *Fusion Relationships* are possessive, totally dependent, jealous. "I can't live without you" is the theme of such an intimate partnership. While the level of commitment here may be valuable, the fusion relationship allows little room for growth of the individual partners. If their personal insecurities and lack of ego strength can be overcome, this bond can produce an arena for maturation. The partners must recognize their interdependence and make opportunities to connect with the world outside their door.

• *Healing Relationships* serve as therapy for one or both individuals. One partner — maybe both — is "on the rebound" from a lost love or an abusive childhood or other disruptive background. The healing relationship may be temporary, having as its primary purpose to salve the wounds of the past, and to help the partner(s) move on when the reconstructive work is finished. A potential hazard is the blow which may come if one partner is committed to someone in need of healing, and is later dumped when the need for help is no longer present.

• *Transitional Relationships* are also short-term. Most people in western cultures go through several as they grow up. Each transitional relationship offers a chance to grow to one's next level of personal maturity and independence. They differ from healing relationships in their focus on "where can we go from here?" to build our individual futures, rather than "how bad my past was." Blinder says the most important growth opportunities in a transitional relationship come when you realize the transitional/growth purpose and make it work for you.

• *Synergistic Relationships* are Blinder's idea of a mature, fulfilling union of two adults who are healthy and grown-up enough for a long-term commitment to one person. The partners have likely experienced one or more of the previous types of relationships, and are now personally prepared to nurture an intimate organism. They may be seen as permanent, authentic, committed. While the partners may expect to continue personal growth throughout their lives, and the relationship can be expected to nurture and sustain that growth, it isn't the purpose of a synergistic relationship to solve problems for one or both partners. They're ready to live fulfilled lives together.

Charting the Shared Purposes of Your Intimate Organism

A close look at the individual Purpose Maps you and your partner create will undoubtedly reveal some *shared* commitment: making the world a better place (e.g. social, environmental, religious, political causes); planning for a family and agreeing on child-rearing direction; educational goals for yourselves and your children; mutual religious commitment; gifts of time and energy to charitable or community causes; personal advancement (making money, getting "ahead").

Now it's time to examine your *mutual* purposes, the aims and goals of your intimate organism *as a partnership*. You can use the same Purpose Map format you and your partner used in the previous exercise. Simply adapt the first — "Self" — column to represent the *partnership's* purposes with regard to the individual partners. For example, one purpose of the organism might be "to help each partner fully develop self-reliance."

Ray and Felicia live a life of religious purpose. They are dedicated believers, active in their church, and committed to living a life consistent with the teachings of their faith. They have regular jobs, and are quite successful in their respective business endeavors (he's an engineer, she's in real estate). Yet every few years, they take leaves — or resign if necessary — to go abroad as missionaries in Third World countries. Their purpose in life is primarily external — service to their God and faith — and they follow it devotedly, and with some sacrifice, since they must periodically abandon lucrative careers to live their religious commitment.

Purpose need not involve religion, of course.

Your own purposes may be *internal* (they contribute primarily to the partners and to the relationship itself); or *external* (they contribute to the larger community and humankind).

Here are some examples of *internal purposes*:

... to remain *attractive* to each other.

... to maintain effective *communication*.

... to renew *commitment* to the relationship.

... to seek *enjoyment* together.

... to maintain mutual *trust*.

... to strive to keep the relationship vital and exciting.

... to keep this relationship as the single most important source of support & nurturance & love in your lives.

... to keep your love alive and well.

... to remove obstacles to your individual and joint happiness.

... to protect yourselves and each other.

... to have ready sexual partners.

... to make money.

... to serve each other's emotional needs.

... to strive for equality in your relationship.

... to maintain and support each other's independence and self-respect.

... to grow in wisdom and emotional maturity.

The following are examples of common *external purposes*:

... to contribute to society.

... to serve God.

... to solve problems in the community.

... to raise a family.

... to work together for peace and social justice.

... to help save the natural environment.

... to do volunteer work in the community.

... to develop a large group of friends.

... to talk with others about your values (social,
political, religious).

... to teach technical skills in a developing country.

... to participate actively in a spiritual community.

... to meet others' social expectations.

... to create music, or art, or another aesthetic medium.

... to "give something back to the world."

You may find that several, a few, or none of the items listed above seem to fit your own relationship purposes. We urge you to jot down your thoughts on the subject in your written "Purpose Map" notebook as you read. You'll find it valuable to work at clarifying the qualities which give purpose to *your* intimate partnership. They may be altruistic or self-centered, practical or idealistic, reachable or distant, stable or changing. However close or far away they may seem, they'll give greater meaning and clearer direction to your life together if from time time you identify them, share them with each other, and come to agreement on those which are most important to the two of you in the months ahead.

A Very Special Purpose:
Your Commitment to Your Relationship

Where does your intimate organism fit in your personal priorities? In Chapter Five, we discussed commitment as one of the key dimensions of intimacy. Your commitment to one another is a central purpose of your relationship. Dedication and devotion to your relationship can — and should — be as important a value as are children, family, social relationships, economic success, individual goals in life, or any other purpose which is meaningful to you.

Your motivation to maintain the relationship and to work at making it even better and more mutually satisfying, of course, is largely dependent upon whether your individual life goals are being met in the partnership.

Paul and Priscilla, the couple discussed earlier in this chapter, have very little sense of commitment to their marriage. They're living parallel lives, each going off to work and coming home to share the chores of subsistence, gaining very little personal or relationship fulfillment. They're committed to their individual success at this point in their lives, but not very committed to each other. Should one or the other require emotional support, it's doubtful whether the partner would be able or willing to supply it. Is their intimate partnership supporting their individual goals? Probably not; the partnership simply allows them to go their separate ways.

Like an individual or a family, a relationship requires nurturance if it is to preserve itself. Commitment to the well-being of your intimate organism should be a high-priority purpose. Purpose in an intimate relationship is bound not by the definitions we can place on the printed page, but by the goals and aspirations of the infinitely complex human beings who created it.

Developmental Stages of Purpose in an Intimate Relationship

Let's look at the development of purpose through the life of a relationship.

Early: Idealism and dreams of changing your world (or even the larger World) are the hallmarks of purpose in the early months and years of an intimate relationship. Particularly with young couples, a youthful combination of energy, naivete, and idealism leads them to pursue lofty goals — personal, relationship, and global.

Idealism can be burdensome, however. Psychologist David Brandt, in his book about expectations and disappointment, *Is That All There Is?*, observes that one of the greatest burdens we place on ourselves is that of *false hope*. It's a set-up for disappointment. Noting that as children we adopt fantasies of a world made perfect by Santa Claus and the Good Fairy, Dr. Brandt observes that many of us cling to those wishes as adults. He identifies three categories of disappointment in the area of relationships: (1) idealized or impossible expectations of your *partner;* (2) false notions about how a *relationship* "ought to be" (e.g. the answer to all your problems; totally successful because the sex is great or the love is strong enough; seen the same by both partners; unchanging over time and circumstances); and (3) unrealistic expectations of *yourself.*

Brandt suggests we can deal effectively with life's inevitable disappointments by ". . .acknowledging the disappointment, feeling and expressing the emotions, sorting out the issues, and reaching acceptance." Actively confronting the blows life deals us — with positive, constructive efforts to accept what's happened and then moving on — is the healthy way to respond to disappointment. Lashing out aggressively or retreating passively are self-defeating responses.

The (often unrealistically) high expectations of the early months and years in a relationship are bound to meet some disappointment as real-world limitations are imposed. Kept in perspective, however, and redirected toward more achievable goals, your enthusiasm and energy won't be wasted.

Anita called a radio show and talked with the on-the-air psychologist about her disappointment — and what she's doing about it: "I'm 29, mother of two, and *I'm my Mom!* I was going to do everything different, avoiding all the mistakes I thought my own Mom made. Now I listen to myself with my kids and I hear Mom's voice! My husband and I have decided to enroll in a parent-education class at the community college. We want to get better at this important job."

Middle: As a relationship matures, and as a couple experiences more of the reality and disillusionment life often has to offer, purpose may be tarnished, and become a hidden dimension in the partnership. "Why bother?" is a common lament from those who have tried to "fight city hall" without success. Their purposes during this stage may turn inward, becoming more centered on self and family concerns.

Yet that's as it should be. At this stage, your family needs are likely to be near their peak. Focusing your purposes around the needs of growing children and the maintenance of your loving partnership and family is appropriate and necessary. You may not be taking direct action to change the world, but the results may be even more far-reaching!

Charlene had hoped to go into the Peace Corps and help "change the world." Now 39, she is a reference librarian with three teen-agers. Although she has a twinge of regret that she didn't get the chance to serve in another country, she says proudly, "My kids have a broader world view in high school than I did when I graduated from the university. Maybe I'll end up changing the world *through them*! I know I've helped hundreds of library patrons to understand the world better — and I think that counts for something."

Late: Idealism and reality tend to blend in the later years of relationship. A delicate balance of personal and societal concerns often results in energy directed toward less global but nonetheless altruistic purposes. With family needs not so pressing — since children may be grown and independent — efforts to make a difference are focused upon personal security, the local community, and other realms in which experience has shown they can succeed within the limits of available time, energy, and resources.

In your later years, of course, you also have less to lose by taking risks aimed at reaching idealistic goals. A tour of duty with the Peace Corps (they do take couples if both have useful skills), a volunteer vacation with Habitat for Humanity, or a commitment to teaching illiterate adults to read or visiting shut-ins or "grandparenting" homeless children — such activities can be enormously rewarding purposes for a mature couple.

Mary Catherine Bateson offers a refreshing perspective on purpose over the life span in her book, *Composing A Life*. The daughter of famed anthropologists Gregory Bateson and Margaret Mead, she proposes that life has *many* beginnings and endings, rather than being a single path toward a pre-set objective. One may achieve various goals — marriage, family, career, social change, artistic — which don't necessarily cohere around a single set of purposes established when one is young and idealistic.

Do maintain clear purposes in your life and in your intimate partnership. But don't lock your "radar" onto a single narrow target for life. Remain flexible, responding to change in your individual needs, those of your partnership and family, and those of the larger community.

Relationship to Other Dimensions

Attraction: Your mutual attraction makes development of and dedication to your purposes much easier. That you like each other and enjoy being together gives you more opportunities for co-creation, and more incentive to work together toward common goals. Your intimate purposes in turn make you even more attractive to each other.

Communication: The process by which purpose is developed and shared, of course, is that of communication. Your partner can't know what you're thinking about unless you make it known. Purposes can be communicated in broad general terms or very specifically. The more specific you are, the more difficult it is to agree. But if you agree, the more likely it is you'll be able to accomplish your purposes. Be sure it's a two-way street, and that your purposes as a couple are shared and agreed upon.

Commitment: Commitment and purpose really do go hand in hand. Coming together and working together in pursuit of common purposes provide the strongest possible foundation for commitment. If your values are shared, if you view the world in a similar way, if you want the same things from life, your paths are parallel, and the chances are great that you can develop a supportive intimate relationship which will help you both to travel your path successfully.

Enjoyment: Creating joy in your life isn't a bad purpose in itself — unless that's *all* you do. Gaining enjoyment from your other activities — work, play, relationships — is a purpose which can both result from and contribute to your "higher" purposes. If their pursuit is enjoyable, you're more likely to go after them with enthusiasm. And if you're enthusiastic, you're more likely to succeed. Don't forget *others* in your pursuit of enjoyment. Bringing joy to the lives of other people is right up there among the highest of purposes.

Trust: Shared values have been shown to be a significant contributing factor in building mutual trust. To the degree that you and your partner hold mutual values and life purposes, you enhance your framework for trusting each other more fully. That trust in turn provides a bond which strengthens you to pursue your life purposes.

On Living Purposefully

Dr. Susan Campbell is a California psychologist whose popular book *The Couple's Journey* discusses purpose in relationship as an evolving sense of oneness with others:

"I have witnessed and guided many intimate journeys. And although every couple is unique, all seem to have at least one thing in common — the search for a sense of meaning:

A sense that their daily individual struggles made sense in some kind of social or global context.

A sense that they could *learn* and *grow* from their experiences rather than repeating the same trials and errors over and over and over.

A sense that they could have an *impact* on their surroundings — on the culture as well as on their partner.

A sense that their life made a *difference*, no matter how small, in the overall scheme of things."

Campbell's "Co-Creation Stage" of *The Couple's Journey* has these key developmental tasks:

"We learn to cooperate with the forces that be toward creating a saner and more humane world.

We become the creators of our own universe.

We experience ourselves as interdependent with all of life."

Building Purpose in Your Intimate Organism

• Give your relationship priority — treat your partner well. That will contribute to your children and the community as well.

• When your intimate organism is successful, it gives back to the larger community, *just because* it's successful. Thus, it isn't selfish to work on improving yourself and your relationship. When you and your intimate relationship are functioning at a high level, you are up, and you'll be more fulfilled, satisfied, successful in other realms of your life, and thus contribute more to others.

• Examine the other five key dimensions of your intimate partnership attraction, communication, commitment, enjoyment, trust — and look for ways each can be strengthened to help build your purpose.

• Set your sights even higher than your real goals. Don't create unrealistic expectations for yourself, but keep in mind that nobody's perfect, so allow for mistakes!

• Remember that neither life nor love are "zero-sum" games. It isn't necessary for someone to lose so the other can win. Both partners can win.

• Check up on yourself with the following exercise, at least once a year:

1. You and your partner each take a piece of standard size writing paper and fold it down the middle (vertically). On the right hand side of the page write down ten words which you believe friends, relatives, and co-workers would use to describe you and your partner *as a couple.* (For example, they might call you "generous," "affectionate," "unsociable.") Edit the list a bit

if you need to, so that it reflects your best estimate of *how others honestly view you*.

2. When you have completed this list, turn the still-folded sheet over, and on the left-hand side write down at least ten words which describe the *ideal couple you would like to be*.

3. Now merge your "others" (step 1) and "ideal" (step 2) lists with those of your partner (no arguments here — accept all ten items on each partner's lists into the merged list) so that you have two new lists: one list (ten-to-twenty items, depending on duplicates) of words which describe how *others* see you, and another list (again ten-to-twenty) of words which describe who you'd *like to be*.

4. What words appear on both of the merged lists? These are the areas in which you're achieving your goals.

5. What words appear on the "ideal" list and not on the "others" list? These are potentially important goals for your relationship.

6. What words appear on the "others" list and not on the "ideal" list? These are messages you're sending to others which may not truly reflect who you want to be.

7. Spend some time with your partner discussing your goals and how (or whether) you want others to see them.

8. Finally, try to assign *rankings* to the goals you and your partner have agreed upon in this exercise. If you can agree upon three or four major goals to go after together, you'll have set a very valuable agenda for your relationship over the next few months (or years!).

 eight

trust

"My Life Is In Your Hands"

The savings and loan crisis, deforestation, the Gulf War, stock market scandals, "Glasnost," Watergate, South Africa, oil spills, crime, discrimination, sexual exploitation, child abuse, spousal abuse — you don't need to look far these days to find a reason not to be trusting.

On a more personal level, partners express their hesitation to trust with pre-nuptial agreements, phone taps, private detectives, even lie detector tests. Remote or personal, these episodes influence our inclinations to trust others — including our partners.

It's not that folks don't want to trust. A recent survey result echoes what most of us are feeling. The Wharton School of Business at the University of Pennsylvania asked more than 3,000 electronics manufacturers to identify the characteristics they wanted most in their sales representatives. *Honesty, integrity,* and *trustworthiness* were the top three selections, on a list of 43 possibilities, outscoring such "bottom-line" traits as competence, product knowledge, and experience. Dare we hope that this study suggests our society is beginning to place greater value on honesty and trustworthiness?

Complex and fascinating, trust isn't an easy concept to depict. Bonds, promises, pledges, and vows, are terms which come to mind. Friends of trust are loyalty, fidelity, integrity, constancy. Enemies of trust are fear, cynicism, suspicion, jealousy. Trust-related issues touch our lives in many ways, positive and negative.

Here are a few comments we've heard from clients who are concerned about trust:

"She's addicted to shopping. I can't trust her. She sniffs out any bargain within a 50-mile radius! Money flows through her hands like water. Trouble is, the well's running dry!"

"If I leave him in charge of the kids, he gets preoccupied. Soon they're out of sight, flirting with danger. I've warned him several times, but it doesn't seem to do any good. It's hard to trust him with them."

"Our daughter has lied to us a few times recently about who she's out with at night."

"He had one affair during our relationship. We worked it out pretty well, but in the back of my mind I wonder if I can really trust him anymore."

"I told my parents about one of our fights and all of a sudden everyone in the family knows."

"She gets so involved in her work and at home that it leaves little time for me. Sometimes I question if she really loves me. Oh, I know if I asked her she'd say yes, but it's what she does that makes me wonder."

"Sometimes I don't follow through as well as I should on things I've promised to do around the house and at work."

As these examples show, trust — of others and of ourselves — cuts a wide path through the intimate landscape.

A Foundation for Trust

You and your partner entered your intimate relationship with a background of life experiences that influenced how much you trust yourselves, each other, and those in your environment. Think of all the ways you learned to trust — or not to trust — from your family, friends, school, religious experiences... from living life! Then consider the very close relationships you had within your original family. Finally, recall your dating or marriage relationships. All those experiences, especially highly positive or negative ones, influence your level of trust in current relationships — including your intimate organism.

Susan was sent to a therapist when she was 17. The therapist manipulated her into having intercourse with him throughout the four months she was in therapy. She never disclosed the information to anyone until she married Allen years later. She did so because she couldn't allow herself to trust Allen as fully as they both would have liked.

Teri's favorite high school teacher, Mr. Dahlstrom, supported her through many trying times, academically and emotionally. He was always ready to listen and give wise counsel. She found that she could trust him completely. Teri continually reflected on what he did for her as she grew older, and tried to use him as a model for her dealings with others.

Rick's first wife had repeated sexual encounters with other men and often "threw it in his face." He had to pull her out of bars, worry about where she was on "lost" weekends, and deal with a variety of other embarrassing incidents. He lost trust in her. When they finally divorced, he felt he could never trust another woman.

When Randy was in junior high, he was handsome, a star athlete, a good student, and very popular with girls. He let it all go to his head. He bragged and flaunted his success. One day a large group of his friends decided to "teach him a lesson." They cornered him, surrounding him so that he couldn't escape, and bombarded him with caustic, critical put-downs. He was completely devastated.

Martha's parents were very trusting throughout her growing-up years. They believed in her, trusted her to make good decisions and were there, when she got into any serious difficulties, to help her learn from those experiences. After she started her own married life, she frequently reflected on the loving, trusting foundation her parents had provided.

These examples suggest how early experiences with trust influence current trust levels. They also lead us to wonder, "What is this thing we call *trust?*"

What Does Trust Mean to You?

We've emphasized throughout this book that the intimate organism is an interrelated system. Like the other dimensions, trust touches each facet of your intimate organism. Attraction loses its fascination without trust; commitment is empty without trust; communication is meaningless without trust; enjoyment has no luster without trust; purpose is lifeless without trust.

Genuine intimacy demands much of us; its most basic demand is that partners must be able to trust each other.

We are speaking of trust in a deep, overall sense. There must be an underlying feeling that your intimate partner can be trusted with your basic being. Without this, your relationship has no foundation.

One way to capture the essence of trust is break it down into the components we deal with day by day. Psychologists John Rempel and John Holmes divide trust into three basic elements: predictability, dependability, and faith.

Predictability refers to being able to tell what your partner's behavior will be in specific situations. Jackie had this to say about Joe: "Joe's like clockwork around the house. He makes breakfast every morning for me and the kids and gives them baths on his duty nights."

Dependability relates to whether you can count on your partner when the need arises, especially when you want to disclose personal feelings and reactions. Clyde told us, "If Bonnie or I have something important to discuss, we know that the other will be willing to treat it seriously and help work it through."

Faith means that you can know your partner will always care for and be responsive to you. Here's Shere on the subject: "George has shown over the years that he'll always love me, no matter what. We've been through some pretty rough times together and been real mad at times, but he always comes back and shows me he really cares despite our difficult times. And he has never broken our vow of being faithful."

So, what would you say if we asked you, "Do you trust your partner?" We hope you'd reply, "In what way?" Your answer surely would depend upon what *stage* your relationship is in and what *dimensions* of your relationship you have in mind when answering!

Trust Through the Stages of a Relationship

Like the other dimensions of an intimate relationship, trust changes over time. Trust issues aren't likely to be at the top of your agenda at the outset, but build in importance as you get to know and care for each other more deeply. Here's a brief summary of how trust develops as an intimate organism grows:

Early Stage. In the beginning you and your partner may be, on one hand, very, very transparent in your trust, and on the other, very protective, holding back. Rare is the couple who have deep, intimate, trust from the start. Indeed, it's nigh on impossible. Trust is built over months and years of successes and failures, through the triumphs and tribulations of a life together.

Middle Stage. Intimate relationships in the middle years are often characterized by "power struggles" — a process of working through toward trust. Partners push and pull, give and take, sorting out how much and in what areas they can trust. A variety of life experiences during the middle years of a relationship puts couples to the test: births, injuries, deaths, emotional happenings, conflicts. As you and your partner deal with these challenges together, you either build or undermine trust.

Late Stage. As an intimate partnership matures, the atmosphere becomes more trusting. You've reached some sort of "plan" — probably unspoken — for dealing with everyday trust issues, and have realized that your overall commitment is firm. Breaches of trust at this stage are more hazardous to a relationship, of course; fortunately they're also less likely. Neither of you is perfect, but you're headed in the right direction — toward greater intimate trust.

Everyday Issues of Trust

Intimate trust can be a big deal — or a little one. Let's consider a few commonplace failures in "everyday" trustworthiness:

* *Irresponsible handling of money.* Overspending; miserliness; not balancing the checkbook properly; telling lies about purchases; loaning money; borrowing money; running up the credit card balance without the partner's knowledge; purchasing unneeded big ticket items; gambling.

* *Not being trustworthy in dealing with children or grandchildren.* Forgetting to give them baths; giving them toys beyond their age level; roughhousing with them; not being aware of potentially dangerous situations when babysitting them; transferring unmet needs to them (such as athletic achievement, sexual exploration, drinking and drug behavior, traveling the world); being too harsh or lenient in disciplining them.

• *Lacking dependability in household duties.* Not doing your share; forgetting to do what you agreed to do; doing a sloppy job; doing the job, but sulking; leaving things undone on purpose; breaking objects by doing things hurriedly; begging off because other things take a higher priority; expecting partner to take care of your duties.

• *Behaving questionably in social situations.* Embarrassing your partner by: falling asleep during plays or movies; belching, burping, passing gas; being long-winded and boring; telling off-color jokes; stuffing yourself, talking about personal issues in front of others. Fawning, flirting, pawing; arguing with others; staying too long or too short.

• *Lack of sensitivity when partner discloses innermost feelings.* Not listening; not caring; giving unwanted advice; yawning and acting bored; condemning; yelling, screaming; not understanding; ridiculing or laughing; trying to force your opinion; calling partner stupid, silly, ignorant; distancing yourself; running away; avoiding feelings and touchy issues.

• *Substance abuse.* Misuse of street drugs, alcohol, prescription drugs, pornography, sweets, food, tobacco.

• *Unsafe driving practices.* Speeding; recklessness; unnecessary risks; driving under the influence of alcohol or other drugs; expressing anger aggressively while driving; not using seat belts; not making sure the children are belted in safely.

You get the picture! Everyday "nuts and bolts" issues may appear unimportant on the surface, but they have a heavy influence on trust levels. If Jack can't trust Lorraine to give quality attention to the children, or Suzanne can't trust Rod to balance the checkbook, things start to get a bit testy around the house.

You may be able to tolerate one or two broken bonds in everyday matters, but trust seriously erodes when it becomes a *series* of violations.

How Do I Trust Me...?

Trust also relates to each of you individually. Can you trust yourself? Do you keep your word with your partner, with others, and with yourself? Are you on time when you say you will be? Do you follow through and complete tasks you agree to handle? If you decide to make a significant behavior change, do you stick to it and accomplish your goal? Not trusting yourself, breaking your own trust, creates confusion, doubt, lack of confidence in yourself and others.

What kind of truster are you? Does one of the following types fit your style?

Naive Truster. You trust no matter what happens. You trust those in authority completely. You don't educate yourself about many key issues in the world because you feel things will work out. "They always have."

Rational Truster. The world is to be looked at logically, not from an emotional standpoint. One must be aware of and ready for the inevitability that others will misuse trust. Reason will save us. We just need to get the right people in control — people who will analyze situations in a rational, step-by-step manner.

Anti-Truster. You're skeptical of most everything: "I don't trust anyone any farther than I can throw them." You generally see the world filled with people who'll take advantage of or use others if they get the chance. You watch for chances to prove your point — and you find plenty of them.

Compassionate Truster. The world needs to change; people are being hurt, and things can change for the better. We need to become involved in transforming the areas where mistrust is being created. We can pursue and conquer and restore the world to a safe, trusting place where we can raise our children without worry and leave our doors unlocked at night.

Intimate Truster. An intimate truster combines some of the qualities of the naive truster, the anti-truster, the rational truster, and the compassionate truster. But the intimate truster goes beyond these four types, adding new qualities of trust. Intimate trust has a pattern of its own, coming from a solid base of the six major dimensions of intimacy. The intimate truster can develop a high level of trust based on openness, self-confidence, and a willingness to be independent and gently confrontive. Intimate trusters monitor their relationships carefully, dealing with both serious and everyday issues before they create problems of trust.

We hope you're on your way to being an intimate truster!

Emotional and Sexual Trust: Jealousy Rears Its Ugly Head

Emotional commitment means "being there" for your partner, making very sure that the time and effort you devote to other activities or people doesn't undermine your own relationship.

Jealous reactions are a sure sign that something is amiss. Jealousy can arise from lots of different partner behaviors. Here are a couple of examples we've heard from couples in counseling:

Mary: "Sure I'm jealous. Wouldn't you be jealous if your husband spent all day working and all night on his computer? He hardly notices I'm in the house. Once I went for an hour-long walk to see if he would miss me. He didn't even know I was gone."

Ed: "When my wife gets on the phone with her women friends, she becomes animated, alive, joking and carrying on. You'd think she had been drinking. I'm embarrassed to admit this, but I feel jealous. She never talks to me that way. I wish she would give me a tenth of that attention."

Intimate partners can be very creative about what makes them jealous. And partners do lots of things which make others wonder about their emotional commitment to the relationship. Yet, as important as everyday irritations can be, one factor stands alone when it comes to maintaining trust and minimizing jealousy, and that one is sexual commitment.

Infidelity is one of the most devastating events that can happen in a relationship. To know or believe that your partner has violated your trust evokes strong emotions and behaviors —internal and expressed. Anger, rage, fear, resentment, depression, and contempt are typical feelings. Yelling, screaming, hitting, sulking, crying, and stomping are common behavioral expressions. Jealousy often leads to the breakup of the relationship; in extreme cases it has meant the death of one or more people involved.

Harry learned from a friend that his wife was having an affair. "When I found out, I was in shock. I couldn't believe that Bev would do that to me. I was devastated. I was crying so hard I couldn't stop. What had happened to us? When I confronted her I kept asking, 'Why? Why? Why?' I couldn't stand being around her or touching her. I took off. I was in no condition to be behind the wheel, but I drove for hours anyway. I went through feeling stupid and naive to wanting to kill her, to wanting to blow up the house."

What should Harry do? That depends on his commitment to the relationship, and his own goals. Certainly there will be a long process of soul-searching, deciding what to do, and "grief work" for Harry — and for Bev. The ideas in the rest of this chapter may help.

Why Do Intimate Partners Violate Trust?

We've identified several sources of trust issues in intimate partnerships. Although knowing "why" will rarely solve the problem, it can help to understand what's going on. Here's a brief look at five likely "culprits":

• One partner has an *emotional or behavioral problem* which creates trust issues for the other. Maybe unresolved childhood conflicts or personality problems; perhaps deeply-ingrained but faulty expectations and/or beliefs about how to behave. The idea here is that it's your partner's problem and you're an innocent victim of his or her irrational hang-ups.

- The problem has to do with your *relationship*. An obvious (or not-so-obvious) signal is being beamed to you. It may be conscious or unconscious. The trust violation could be a pay back: "You did something bad to me, I'll do something bad to you." Or it could be a *wake-up call*:

"Wake up, you've been ignoring me or treating me poorly."

"Read my actions, I'm not getting my needs met."

"Sleepyhead, you're smothering me. I need more freedom."

- The problem may be a *momentary lapse*:

"My workload has been horrendous, so I actually do *need* to work late for weeks on end."

"He's so interesting, has a magnetic personality, is so easy to talk to."

"I got caught up in the moment. It was a magical evening. She was beautiful, we were far away from home, there was music, wine. . . All of a sudden, we were in bed."

- You have a *jealousy* problem. You've got hang-ups from the past or role expectations or are easily hurt. You may be signaling any of the "culprits" mentioned above: "I'm getting even by being jealous." "I'm jealous because you're not paying enough attention to me." "I've been sick or drunk or depressed about work, so I'm jealous; ordinarily I wouldn't be, and it's not important."

- *Projection* is another spark which may cause a jealousy fire (this one is suggested by marital therapist/author Bruce Fisher). The *other* partner may be the one who is really upset and feeling jealous (or even having an affair), but instead of acknowledging it, puts it off on you by saying, "You're jealous aren't you?" or "Are you having an affair?" This behavior may be self-protective.

What Do You Expect, Anyway?

Broken trust is one of the most difficult tests of a relationship; how to deal with it depends on the severity of the break. An affair is bound to cause a deeper wound than failure to do the laundry, although chronic breaks of "everyday" trust can cut deeply.

Violations of trust often result when both partners don't clearly understand what's expected. Your *expectations* for each other's behavior are in your heads, and if you don't spell them out aloud, you can *expect* trouble.

Jacob and Geri are a couple whose expectations became a real source of conflict. Jacob grew up without any responsibilities at home. Everything was done for him. In Geri's family the boys cared for the animals, washed dishes, cleaned their rooms, and picked up after themselves. Geri expected Jacob to do these things just as her brothers had. Unfortunately, she didn't say so out loud. When Jacob allowed the dog to run away while she was gone, Geri became extremely upset. She felt he had violated her trust. He understood her concern for the dog, but didn't see the unfortunate event as a breach of trust.

Be careful that your assumptions and expectations are out in the open and discussed. Once that hurdle is cleared, you can deal with the broken trust by using good communication skills to tackle the next major issues: acceptance and forgiveness. Monitor your relationship carefully, and talk out everyday trust issues on a continuous basis, as "routine maintenance" for your intimate organism.

Rebuilding Trust: After the Fall

Perhaps it goes without saying that the impact of a sexual affair on an intimate partnership can be devastating. The ultimate decision must be made: whether or not the relationship will end. The level of hurt is extreme, with much mental confusion and emotional turmoil. The grieving process, the rebuilding process, and the road to recovery are long and difficult. The process of healing an intimate relationship after an affair will take a considerable time — perhaps several years.

Change is the major path to renewal of broken trust. The violator must work very hard to re-establish credibility. The process will require extraordinary demonstrations of fidelity, dependability, and repentance toward the offended spouse. Apologies must show in actions as well as in words, and must be accompanied by sincere efforts to repair the relationship. Such efforts will be unique to each situation, of course, but here are a few possibilities:

- Appropriately sincere verbal apologies;
- Renewed focus of time and energy on the primary intimate partnership;
- Taking on additional responsibilities at home;
- Occasional spontaneous acts of giving (a hand-crafted gift for no particular occasion, a "day off" from chores for the partner);
- Completion of long-avoided home projects;
- Dependability in fulfilling obligations (household chores, being on time);
- Special mini-vacations or short trips to places *the partner* especially enjoys;
- Paying unusually careful attention to what the partner has to say (and to the underlying feelings).

Keep in mind that the central core of this process is the *sincerity* of the trust-violator's efforts. *What* you do is less important than is *how* you do it. Flowers sent automatically by the florist every Friday will be meaningless after a couple of weeks. Whistling while you spontaneously — and unbidden — wash the windows on a Saturday will be noticed. Efforts to make amends must come from the heart. You're lucky if you're given a second chance — consider it as if you're starting a new courtship from scratch.

There are no easy solutions to problems of infidelity. Good communication skills (see Chapter Four) are appropriate, but the depth of work needed goes far beyond the basics. It's very likely in these circumstances that you'll need to seek out a professional counselor or therapist to help you work through this difficult problem.

But don't expect a therapist to say simply, "He's wrong and he's got to shape up. . . " *The intimate organism is a system.*

It Takes Two. . .

Most affairs have something to do with the offendee as well as the offender. If *your* partner has cheated, that's a tough one to handle — and it's one of the most difficult concepts of intimacy to understand. Nevertheless, it's a fact: *both partners contribute to any problem within the relationship.* It may not be equal, 50-50, but when a problem arises, you each contribute something to the development of the problem and to the maintenance of the problem. You *as a couple* keep the problem alive by your current actions, and you helped cause it by your behavior in months and years past. *The intimate organism is a system.*

This is tricky ground to tread. Even though your partner may have had an anger problem or a drinking problem or a jealousy problem long before you became intimate partners, when you two became intimately involved, you became *co-creators* of that problem in its current form.

Relationships and families in which chemical dependency is a problem, for instance, often fail to acknowledge the role non-using intimates play in keeping the dependency going. "Co-dependent" and/or "enabler" roles may result from ignorance, or naivete, or well-meaning efforts to "help," or fear of outside intervention, or any of a dozen other motivations. No matter the reasons. The *result* is always the same: the dependent person has an ally who helps keep the dependency going.

The process works in the same way with other undesired behavior patterns in intimate systems. The way you respond to each other or get caught up with each other in the problem helps keep it alive. You create it together. Who knows why? Perhaps both of you need to learn lessons; perhaps you can help each other to new levels of growth; perhaps it's dumb bad luck; perhaps we'll never know the exact reason. But there it is in front of you to deal with — if you choose to do so. You are both intimately involved in the problem and — we hope — in the solution.

"Spontaneous affairs" do happen, but they're the exception. Much more often a couple has a history of attempts to deal with issues before an affair actually took place. The attempts may have been direct or indirect; rarely are they in the form of a bottom-line threat ("If we don't solve this problem, I'll have an affair"). Among couples we've worked with in therapy, affairs usually follow long-term frustration, and a series of dead-end attempts at resolution.

Ron and Alice are a good example. They had an ongoing battle over how to bridge their different communication styles. Alice didn't like to fight overtly, in the sense of "letting it all hang out." Ron preferred a "good fight," full of raised voices, harsh words, aired complaints about each other, and a passionate reconciliation. Alice's withdrawal at any hint of a fight only made Ron pursue her more actively in order to seek resolution. After years of this unsatisfying pattern, Ron eventually drifted into an affair with a co-worker whose style was much more open.

Whose problem was it? Both Ron and Alice had something to do with creating the affair. We're not trying by any means to excuse the affair or take Ron off the hook. He and he alone made the choice to have the affair. But Alice was a *contributor* (even if unintentional), and if those two are going to stay together and work out their mutual problem, *both* will need to change. Regardless of the how and why of what took place, they both must take responsibility. Together they created the conditions which led Ron to the affair, and together they must establish the new conditions which can lead to successful resolution of the problem.

If you can come to accept the idea that both of you share responsibility for the situation that led to an affair, it may be easier to think about forgiveness. If you both decide to stay in the relationship, there must be forgiveness at some point. It need not necessarily be spoken; but for the heart to heal, only an act of forgiveness will lift the burden you both share.

Recovery from a severe break of trust is always painful, always difficult, never comfortable. Nevertheless, there is hope. Here are some specific *cooperative* steps which can help heal the wounds and rebuild a healthy intimate partnership:

• Both partners acknowledge that the responsibility for broken trust is shared. A breakdown occured in their *system* — the intimate organism itself — not just in one guilty partner.

• The partner who took the trust-breaking step (e.g., the one who had the affair) must accept responsibility for having made the choice to violate trust. Although the intimate system may have been flawed, no one was *forced* to go astray.

• The partner who feels "wronged" must withhold condemnation, and at least be willing to *consider* forgiveness.

• The "trust breaker" must take firm, positive steps to demonstrate renewed dependability, loyalty, and commitment to the relationship. (The suggestions on page 125 are a good beginning.)

• The partners can begin to improve their open communication about the problems which led to the breach of trust, including assumptions and expectations.

• The partners can do a thorough assessment of the six dimensions of their intimate organism, and begin to work together to strengthen each dimension, perhaps with the help of a qualified couples therapist.

• The partner who remained trustworthy can eventually forgive.

Self-Disclosure As a Builder of Intimate Trust

Many researchers and writers on intimacy speak of trust primarily in terms of knowing each other well and trying hard to understand each other's viewpoints. Intimate awareness and understanding grow as you live your lives together and carefully observe what each other does. You gain intimate knowledge by dealing with issues when they arise and by having discussions about the relationship. Willingness to gently confront each other when the need arises helps you to know and understand each other better and to build trust. Intimate self-disclosure also leads to a special knowledge and understanding of your partner that few others get to see. Knowing someone on these levels below the surface fosters a special caring and reciprocal trust.

We would like to add a caution about "intimate self-disclosure," however. Many authors in the field of intimacy hold up self-disclosure as the ultimate key to creating intimacy. It is our belief that *self-disclosure is only one small part of total intimacy*. Texas philosophy professor Robert C. Solomon, the author of *About Love*, offers these thoughtful comments on this subject:

"We too often read that intimacy is 'the ability to reveal innermost feelings, thoughts and emotions to someone else without becoming anxious or afraid' and 'to reveal yourself without fear of reprisal.'. . . The idea that intimacy is self-revelation is one-sided, as if intimacy is an act that one person does to (or at) another instead of an experience shared. It also tends to put too much emphasis on verbal expression, on confession, on conversation. The focus on revelation — the transfer of embarrassing information to a willing and sympathetic listener — misses the point of intimacy."

Professor Solomon's view offer much-needed balance to the popular notion that self-disclosure is the key to intimacy. If used to meet your selfish need to "confess" a real or imagined sin, it can be the key to the exit door.

Building Trust: An Ounce of Prevention

Can couples prevent trust issues from forming in the first place? Not entirely, perhaps. We're only human after all. But there are preventive steps which can help you and your partner develop a solid foundation of trust in your intimate system.

- Most of the time you get back what you give in intimate

relationships. If you can be trusted to do what you say, and you're consistently cooperative and helpful in dealing with your partner, your action will help build trust. It will serve as an example your partner is likely to follow in dealing with you. "If you go the extra mile for me, I'll do it for you." The power of *being trustworthy* is greatly underestimated as a trust builder. Sure, there are risks, but if you're going to be trusted, you must trust. (Naive trusters, take special care, but don't stop trusting!)

• Here's a trust-building idea that sounds simpler than it is. *Paying attention* means watching for and listening to the "signals" your partner puts out. These signals can be verbal or nonverbal, direct or subtle. When you or your partner have feelings of distrust — like feeling left out or neglected or jealous — you usually put out signals. Even before affairs happen, there is often a long history of signals that haven't been noticed or resolved satisfactorily. Pay attention, learn to deal with them constructively, and these signals will help you know and understand each other better.

• The power of *dialogue* in building a base of trust in your relationship can't be overstated. Marital experts universally place communication as the cornerstone of a healthy, trusting partnership. Their voices chant in unison the "secret" to creating intimate trust: "communication," "communication," "communication." To build trust requires that you take time to monitor the signals of your relationship and to talk about potential obstacles to trust whenever you become aware of them.

• Kerry Hart of General Motors Corporation has identified three steps necessary for building organizational trust: *openness and congruity; shared values;* and *autonomy and feedback.* These ideas are applicable to intimate trust as well. Be honest and open. Mean what you say, and say what you mean. Communicate your purposes and values in the relationship so you're both heading in the same direction. Respect each other's individuality. Give each other ongoing feedback about how you're treating each other day-in-and-day-out.

• Changing your attitude and being assertive are recommended by Radford Williams, author of *The Trusting Heart*. He offers three suggestions in order to accomplish a trusting heart: reduce your cynical mistrust of the motives of others; reduce the frequency and intensity with which you experience emotions such as anger, irritation, frustration, rage; learn to treat others with kindness and consideration; and develop your assertiveness skills for unavoidable situations.

Finally, here are three ideas from psychologists John Remple and John Holmes:

• Don't overinterpret negative behavior from the past. Thinking about past negative events makes you insensitive to your partner's present actions. Don't judge based on the past.

• Focus on specific, concrete behavior. Don't jump to harsh conclusions about your partner's motives and character.

• Be more sensitive to and appreciative of positive behavior. Give your partner credit and some room to make mistakes. Try to believe in your partner even when you're uncertain.

To Trust or Not To Trust?

Intimate trust is built slowly. Broken trust is rebuilt even more slowly. Commitment, patience, mutual respect, purpose, communication, and love are the key ingredients of trust. It's a precious, delicate quality. If you lack it, get busy building it. If you have it, treat it with the greatest care.

nine

intimacy respects individuality

"Let there be spaces in your togetherness"
— Kahlil Gibran

"Intimacy, relationship, partnership, . . . love, caring, commitment, . . . partner, spouse, mate, . . . *WHAT ABOUT ME?* I'm feeling swallowed up by all this *togetherness*. I need room to be a person, and I want my partner to respect my *separateness!*"

How can you maintain your individual identity within your intimate organism? After all, the rest of the world looks at the two of you as a couple. Your partner wants you to put the relationship first. You even have expectations of yourself as half of an intimate pair.

Yet there are genuine differences between you. You're both unique, individual persons. And, like all intimate partners, you'll often disagree about matters of conduct, interests, values, beliefs, hobbies.

Is there a way to work out such differences so that your individual needs and preferences are respected without undermining your relationship?

" . . .Once the realization is accepted that even between the *closest* human beings infinite distances continue to exist," advises poet Rainer Maria Rilke, "a wonderful living side by side can grow up . . ."

"You Light Up My Life"

Candle-lighting ceremonies have long been a traditional feature of church weddings. Two of three candles are lighted at the beginning of the ceremony; a larger middle candle remains unlit until the marriage vows are completed. Then the partners both hold up their flames to light the center candle, symbolizing the start of a new life together. At that point, the traditional ritual calls for them to blow out their individual candles — signifying that the separate partners are now one.

As it happens, both of us attended such weddings while writing this chapter. We enjoyed the candle-lighting ritual *until the individual candles were snuffed out.* We applaud the interdependence/oneness concept represented by the center candle, but blowing out the individual candles suggests to us that the new partners must give up their independence and autonomy completely — to snuff it out. We'd like to see the newlyweds light a joint candle together and then *leave their respective individual candles still burning!* This variation of the traditional ritual would signal continuing respect for the full capabilities and individuality of each partner *as well as* creation of a new intimate organism with the potential to achieve much more than either partner alone.

In joining together two independent persons to form one interdependent love partnership, there will be some sacrifice of autonomy or individuality, but it shouldn't be total annihilation! A marriage that is so intertwined that it suffocates individual feelings and talents and ideas is destined not to live up to its full potential.

"Mature love," says famed psychoanalyst Erich Fromm, "is union under the condition of preserving one's integrity, one's individuality."

We want to help you *celebrate* your individuality and your partner's — to use your healthy intimate organism as a basis for greater fulfillment of yourselves as unique individual human beings. Remember that the intimate organism is a living system — its changes affect both of you and its health is capable of sustaining you in your individual well being.

Throughout this book, up to this point, we've emphasized nurturing your intimate organism. Now it's time to consider how your intimate organism can return the favor by nurturing the two of you as individuals. The rest of this chapter offers some practical tools for enhancing — and celebrating — the individuality of each partner.

Understanding Your Individuality

There are myriad differences between individuals, of course. No two people are alike. Some of those differences are important to intimacy; others are not. A few of the more important ones include:

Early history (centered around your families of origin, childhood, friendships, and other early relationships);

Cognitive styles (your ways of looking at the world; e.g. rational vs. emotional);

Social styles (preference for involvement with others vs. solitude);

Self-esteem (belief in yourself vs. self-doubt);

Openness to new experiences (interest in "what's out there" in the world vs. preference for the known and familiar);

Standards of judgement (rigid vs. flexible approach to evaluating "right" and "wrong");

Self-awareness (knowing your own feelings, beliefs, attitudes vs. uncertainty, lack of awareness);

Existential perspective (preference for living now, "one day at a time," vs. focusing on the past or future);

Sensitivity to others (ability to recognize and respond to feelings in others vs. insensitivity or lack of perception);

Time consciousness (living by the clock vs. relaxed "take it easy" style);

Assertiveness (uninhibited constructive self-expression vs. shy reserve or hurtful aggression);

Individual communication styles (open verbal expressiveness vs. indirect or nonexpressive or overpowering approaches); and

Beliefs, attitudes, values (social attitudes, prejudices, religious beliefs, political ideas, human values).

Two people with unique heredities, environments, health and psychological histories, thinking styles, personalities, ways of self-expression, interests and talents are bound to have some important differences!

We encourage you to spend time understanding your own and your partner's individuality. Doing so will give you a clearer perspective for viewing each other's behavior. Insights gained can help you support and encourage each other's ways of expressing individuality, develop hidden or rusty individual potential, discuss and negotiate individuality issues, and accommodate and accept unique qualities which do not change.

We're not going to enter the debate whether various individual differences are due to heredity or environment. Such arguments are ancient, ongoing, and controversial; and we're not going to resolve them here. We're trying to stay practical. For purposes of this discussion, we've grouped individual differences into three key categories which are particularly important for understanding each partner's individuality: your *early family experiences;* your *prior relationship experiences;* and your *attitudes, beliefs, and expectations* about intimacy.

• Start with your *early family experiences.* How did your

mother and father, siblings, and relatives help create your individuality? Sketch your "family tree," and make an effort to talk or correspond with living members with whom you're not in regular contact. Ask about their views of the family, "skeletons" in the family closet, obscure relatives whose stories have been lost or forgotten. Pay particular attention to details about your parents and siblings.

Discuss and share family histories with your love partner. See if the two of you can identify family patterns on either side which influence your individual styles in relating to one another, or key attitudes in other areas (e.g., money management, child rearing, home organization), or real or potential expressions of individual talents and desires.

Explore your early upbringings in terms of education, interests, hobbies, talents, spirituality, and other factors important to you. Are there special experiences or people other than your family of origin that influenced your individuality? Perhaps your experiences as a member of the debate team or with a special friend (or enemy!), or your participation in church helped form you in certain ways.

• *Previous intimate relationships* can be particularly important in shaping your individuality in your current relationship. (The results can be negative or positive.) Maybe you learned to sulk and pout to get what you wanted, or to be super cautious about expressing what you want, or to make accusations at the slightest hint of trouble. You might have learned how to budget and spend money wisely, or to speak up before things got out of hand, or to present a united front when disciplining the children. Past intimate experiences are fertile ground to till when looking for (positive or negative) issues to be discussed. Help each other enhance the positive and work through the negative expressions of your individuality.

• Silent *attitudes, beliefs, and expectations* about how intimacy should work come from many quarters. Family of origin, upbringing, peers, previous relationships, gender role conditioning, the media, and religious teachings are only some of the many ways your view of intimacy is shaped. They all contribute to your unique way of expressing individuality within your intimate organism. Attitudes, beliefs, expectations may be inside your head, but they usually are readily detected through watching your behavior and listening to what you say.

Here are some common attitudes, beliefs and expectations which many couples stumble over:

• You feel that it's good to discuss areas of disagreement openly.

• You expect both you and your partner to have equal rights throughout your relationship.

• You believe that much time should be devoted to understanding diet and preparing healthy meals.

• You feel that children are people too, should be able to express their rights and opinions openly, and should get their needs met.

• You believe that sexual foreplay isn't necessary, that both partners can be ready to "perform" quickly.

• You expect to have a lot of alone time in your relationship, a chance to get away from each other.

• Your attitude toward birthdays, anniversaries, and holidays is nostalgic and sentimental. You buy cards and gifts and do other special caring things.

• Traditional religion, from your viewpoint, is severely limited. Regular church services have little appeal for you.

Whether these or similar situations will undermine or enhance your intimate relationship — and your individual uniqueness — depends on how each partner approaches the issue involved. Can you accept or accommodate such differences? How important are they, really? Can you agree upon changes which one or both of you need to make? How do you handle disagreement? Are you treating each partner's individuality equally? How much room is there for individual expression in your partnership?

Explore each position carefully, learn more about each other's ideas so that you can help each other develop further. Establish equality as your basic rule, and use the communication tools in Chapter Four to work toward a mutually satisfactory solution.

Here's another way to look at these issues of individuality: The U.S.A. has succeeded as an experiment in democracy to the extent that it has allowed for and enhanced the enormous variety and range of backgrounds, lifestyles, needs, opinions, and other differences of its citizens. Perhaps that respect for the individuality of two-hundred million persons in a society isn't a bad model for accommodating the individual differences of the two partners in an intimate organism!

Developing Mutual Respect, Self-Esteem, and Equality

Mutual respect involves recognizing and honoring your own and each other's equal value as persons, along with the value of your relationship. You can demonstrate that respect by giving special attention to yourself, your partner and your relationship, holding each of these in high esteem.

Psychologist C. Edward Crowther has this to say about mutual respect between intimates:

" . . . with respect, a relationship brings new opportunities. There's so much you can learn from one another. There are so many more experiences you can have because each person enriches the other's life, opens new doors, brings new perspective. You find yourself constantly impressed with the other person's intelligence, thoughtfulness, kindness, sensitivity, beauty, grace, handsomeness."

When both partners have solid self-esteem, you can build a stronger intimate relationship. If you and your partner like and respect yourselves, if you feel adequate in dealing with most life situations, if you're both confident that you're valuable human beings, you have a great deal to give to your partnership.

In turn, a strong and vital intimate partnership will enhance the self-worth of each of the partners — another example of *reciprocity* in the intimate relationship.

Respecting each other does not mean giving up yourselves. Nor does it mean sacrificing everything for your partner — although you're likely to be *willing* to do that for the one you love most. True intimacy is mutually fulfilling. You're proud of each other's achievements, at the office or at the stove, in the garage or in the community, with the children or with the company, on the playing field or on the street.

Both partners commit their full energies to a truly intimate relationship, and in turn are nurtured by it. All three components — the two individuals and the partnership — grow stronger as a result. Good partner self-esteem enhances an intimate organism, and a stronger intimate organism improves the self-esteem of the partners.

University of Texas professor Robert Solomon puts it clearly:

"Love that lasts, ultimately, is love that mutually maximizes self-esteem. Love that fails, love that falls apart, is passion or companionship that leaves the self untouched or worse, that degrades the self and renders the shared self something less than it was before love came along."

In recent years, "equality" between the sexes has been commonly understood to refer to the struggle of women for parity in economic rewards, job opportunities, political power, access to influence, sexual relationships, and self-determination. In the context of the intimate organism, equality suggests a balance of rights and responsibilities, no dominant partner, shared decision making, equal self-respect, and self-esteem.

Mutual respect is an absolute essential in intimate partnerships. Valuing your partner, honoring your partner's ideas, supporting your partner, gracefully accepting each other's differences, tolerating disagreement without being disagreeable, actively listening when your mate has something to say — all these are part of this vital component of a healthy intimate organism.

"In loving relationships," note University of Maryland philosophers Douglas MacLean and Claudia Mills," people not only find intimacy, they also discover new ways to step on each other's toes, violate each other's dignity, and show a lack of respect . . . If justice isn't the focus of loving relationships, it must still be a continuing concern."

Fred and Lucy build each other's self-esteem by listening when the partner is talking, by encouraging each other's career advancement, by supporting each partner's independence and self-expression. Ethel and Rick, in contract, ignore each other's requests, criticize each other in front of friends and family, make fun of each other's career ambitions. Guess which relationship is on the rocks?

Justice, dignity, and mutual respect aren't automatic. They require conscious effort — and rededication to the principles of equality of intimate partners.

High self-esteem is a valuable personal asset. It can be developed, and it doesn't require money, or power, or beauty, or a great job. What it does involve is a commitment to yourself, a willingness to accept who you are as a foundation for becoming who you want to be, and the effort to work at your own growth in self-expression, self-confidence, and self-valuing. It isn't selfish, because the result of healthy self-esteem is greater capacity and willingness to share yourself and your abilities with others.

Keep in mind that we're speaking here of honest self-esteem, enduring belief in your value as a human being. We're most emphatically *not* endorsing the sort of of *braggadocio* which says, "I'm the greatest!" You *are* a lovable, valuable person regardless of your strengths and (inevitable human) weaknesses. We hope you believe in yourself, that you esteem yourself enough to take care of the valuable human being you are!

Negotiating and Compromising About Individuality Issues

Individuality shows itself in concrete ways in intimate organisms. Your unique qualities usually come to the forefront — unless you've learned to suppress the real you "for the sake of the relationship." How do you march to your own drummer, express your individual thoughts, feelings, and behaviors in relationship to your partner? What would you do in the following situations?

• You give a lot of energy to a special hobby. Your partner complains that you spend too much time at it, to the neglect of other important matters.

• You discover that you and your partner handle money differently. One believes that money is meant to flow in and out, without much attention to how it is spent. The other is more miserly, believes in saving and budgets, and watches every penny.

• When you and your partner meet new couples, you get along fine — for a few months. Soon your partner starts to "educate" the other couple about everything, going into a "know-it-all" lecture mode. Many couples have dropped by the wayside over the years, and you're becoming quite concerned.

These are real differences of real people in real intimate relationships. While it is important that partners respect and esteem each other's individuality — and maybe even some "weirdness" — there are times when it's necessary to bring up feelings of disagreement, concern, and fairness in order to set the stage for compromise.

Instead of remaining silent or expressing yourself nonverbally about individuality issues like these, we urge you to bring them out in the open. It's important to talk about the issue without making critical or blaming statements.

Refresh yourself on the good communication skills from Chapter Four, and practice them as you work out an equitable solution. The negotiation-compromise process is particularly important in fostering equality, working things out in a balanced way, and allowing for graceful acceptance of differences. Try not to get discouraged with the negotiation process. It may take many discussions over a period of months — even years — to work things out. Don't give up, keep trying. Avoid the trap of saying, "We'll never reach a satisfactory resolution to our differences."

Keep these additional suggestions in mind when working toward compromise:

• *Bring your partner into your individual activities whenever feasible and desirable.* "Hey honey, do you want to climb Mount Everest with me this time?"

• *Pay close attention to the practical realities of your life when expressing yourself.* Child rearing, household and work duties can't simply be ignored. "Sorry, boss. The surf was up yesterday, and it completely slipped my mind that I was supposed to be at work."

• *Sacrificing your unique needs in order to preserve your intimate relationship may be in order at times.* "I've decided to give up macrame' because I know it offends you."

• *Don't undermine your intimate relationship in order to have your own way.* "I demand, insist, require that you accept my need to sleep under the bed."

• *Be prepared to sacrifice your own individuality on occasion* to help further the more socially or economically valuable qualities of your partner. "I just got offered a million dollar salary in Hawaii, but I'm required to work twelve-hour days and every other weekend for a year. Are you willing to give it a try?"

• *Bargain openly at times about ways you and your partner express — or want to express — each one's uniqueness.* Try to be equal about individuality. "You take Wednesday for basket-weaving and I'll take Monday for hackey-sack."

• *Seek out a competent couple counselor if you reach a stalemate* over issues of being unique individuals. "I've heard about these two great counselors out in California. Let's go!"

Encouraging and Supporting Individuality

Think about a time when someone encouraged and supported your individuality. Remember how nice it felt? Encouragement and support feel like a magic balm! They uplift you, make you feel important, help you dream big dreams and believe in yourself. The person who supported you probably saw into your deeper nature and recognized the untapped potential there.

Wouldn't it be nice if you were more encouraging and supportive with your self and with your partner in terms of individuality? It's helpful to have at least two advocates — yourself and your partner. Individuality can start to shine for both of you. Celebrate yourselves!

Exploring Your Individuality: An Exercise in Self-Discovery

1. In what ways are you a unique individual?
2. What constructive steps can you take to express your individuality more fully?
3. How do your individual qualities (and your partner's) get in the way of your relationship?
4. How do you encourage or discourage your partner's uniqueness?
5. What are some key ways you and your partner can build up your individual self-esteem through your intimate organism?
6. Any irrational ideas about how life together "should" be lurking around in your relationship?
7. How are you teaching your children to develop their own individuality?

Start this quest together. Analyze your own and each other's individuality in terms of the categories we described earlier in this chapter (pages 135 and 136). Do it with a sense of encouragement and support for your current individuality and for areas that are rusty — your latent areas of potential. Discuss ways you could be more encouraging and supportive. Perhaps both of you could listen better to your own inner stirrings about individuality or to your partner's. Maybe you need to be more openly interested or excited when your partner expresses individuality. Have you shown enthusiasm about your partner's new hobby? Have you accompanied her to events, or given a magazine subscription, or held the flashlight, or read up on the subject, or otherwise shown that what's important to him matters to you, too?

There are numerous ways to encourage and support individuality in yourself, your partner, your relationship. Here are a few ideas to get your celebratory juices flowing:

• If your intimate relationship is in a delicate, tenuous state, *build up your "couple immunity base"* — a strong foundation of the six dimensions of your intimate organism — before either of you ventures too far into individual pursuits. "The doctor says the sonogram shows triplets. How about putting off your idea of mining for gold in Alaska?"

• *Develop partnership activities and routines which honor each of you as individuals,* supporting each partner's interests and needs. He can learn to enjoy her quilt exhibit just as she can find pleasure in his sports car show. "I know you're gonna *love* this . . ."

• *Consider — both of you — expressing your individuality in a broader range of activities.* The available range is endless. "On page 659 of *Everything You Always Wanted to Know About Individuality* I see an activity I can try."

• *Respect your partner's individual uniqueness* — even the "weirdness." Don't criticize unfairly or make fun of activities, interests or habits which are important to him or her. "I really enjoy your musical saw!"

• Brainstorm and *expand the ways you can express your uniqueness as a couple.* "Isn't it amazing that neither of us ever learned to play tiddlywinks before? It's such fun!"

Maintain your rights to negotiate and compromise. Just because you're encouraging and supportive doesn't mean that you won't disagree and question the validity or timeliness of an expression of individuality on occasion.

Developing your own sense of self in constructive ways can enliven your relationship and make your togetherness stronger. Draw out, encourage, and support each other's individuality and constructive forms of self-expression. Each person has a highly distinctive nature. Nurturing the individuality of each partner will pay big dividends in the health of your intimate system. It's one of the most rewarding and fulfilling things you can do for yourselves and your relationship.

"I've Tried Everything, But It's No Use"

We know it's not easy. "Individuality" can, after all, get pretty weird at times. Your partner may have turned out to be much more — or less — than you bargained for.

You know by now that our approach to dealing with individuality and other relationship issues emphasizes acceptance, tolerance, communication, negotiation, problem solving, compromise, equality, striving to do the best you can. Still, we know that such a "hang in there" approach will not always work in the real world of intimacy. On occasion, we hear comments — such as these from workshop participants — that cause us to reconsider:

"What if one partner tries harder to make things work or gives more to the relationship than the other? I do all the communicating. I monitor our relationship. I care. I talk. But there is little in the way of response on the other end. And, of course, there's never any type of initiation by my partner."

"In our relationship, I'm the pursuer when it comes to sex. My partner simply isn't as interested as I am. We've tried to communicate, but there's little lasting change."

"I raise the kids by myself, basically. After we discuss my concerns, my partner will help them with their homework for a day or two, or speak with them about completing their chores, or pay them a bit of attention. But soon it all goes by the wayside and I end up doing it all."

The basic complaint in these examples is that of individual differences based on an *inequality*: one partner wants more or is more "into" the relationship — or parts of it — than the other. A variety of solutions may have been tried, from direct, positive or negative communication, to problem solving attempts, to such indirect approaches as giving up. All such efforts are offered in the hope that the partner will respond, fill the gap, change as desired. Yet, repeated attempts at a solution have garnered no response, or a half-hearted or inadequate response, or short-term change, or perhaps active rebellion. The result is that things revert back to the way they used to be. You two are at a stalemate . . . again. Can your intimate organism tolerate the possibility that this problem between you may never be satisfactorily resolved?

Is there any hope in such a situation? It isn't going to be resolved overnight, but here are several possible approaches: 1. Step back and reflect; 2. Start again — perhaps from a different perspective; 3. Try to accommodate; 4. Try acceptance; 5. Give an ultimatum. 6. Get professional help.

Let's take a look at each of those alternatives.

• *Step back and reflect.* Take some time to think deeply about the problem. First, look at yourself. Are you certain your analysis and your motivation are correct? When you're emotionally upset, it's easy to lose perspective. Check out the approaches you have already tried. Many who have reached an impasse haven't exhausted all possibilities because of fear (such as hurting the feelings of the partner) or false expectations (such as expecting that the partner "knows" how to remedy the complaint without further input). In addition, previous attempts may have been presented in a manner which was too demanding or aggressive. None of these approaches will produce the desired outcome.

After you've taken a good look at your own actions in the situation, consider your partner's viewpoint and life circumstances carefully. Maybe other life events are causing interference. Childrearing duties, work responsibilities, family health concerns, or other worries may be blocking full attention to the problem. Put yourself more completely into your partner's shoes and look at the problem from that vantage point.

Have you truly considered the complexities of the problem? Psychologist Robert Weiss speaks of a "sentiment override" in couples who are dealing with conflict areas. He says partners believe they have perfect knowledge of each other; that is, they think they know the "whole story" behind the difficulty. Such preexisting private expectations or beliefs override an objective view of the current difficulty. Things often aren't what they seem in intimate interactions. So slow down, and try to look more deeply within yourself and your partner . . . as objectively as possible.

• *Start again.* After carefully considering the entire situation from new perspectives, it might be good to begin afresh. New attitudes and ideas may allow you actually to overcome the problem. Miracles do happen!

• *Try to accommodate.* Decide to give in. No longer actively resist this particular aspect of individuality. Drop your dispute, but not your disagreement. Let it be known that you still aren't happy with this particular expression, but that you see no sense in negotiating over it any longer. Realize that this expression of individuality won't change. It's simply an area of difference between you, but you don't have to love it.

• *Try acceptance.* Take a deep breath, acknowledge that things aren't going to change, and give up completely. Accept this part of your partner cheerfully. Analyze your commitment and purpose in the overall relationship once again. Take the pressure off by fully accepting and supporting the troublesome factor, without any reservations or recrimination.

You may — reluctantly and after much soul-searching — decide to give up part of your own individuality in order to help your relationship function better and to accept your partner's differences. Such a decision ought not be reached lightly; you'll want to exhaust all the previous options first. Acceptance requires long and sometimes painful discussion, negotiation, and self-introspection.

Equality in a relationship requires a good deal of acceptance; your commitment to equality allows acceptance to come more easily.

• *Give an ultimatum.* You've reached the end of your rope. Nothing has worked, and you're ready to risk it all to solve the problem. *Proceed with caution!* You might say, "I love you, and I'm ready to do my part, but this can't go on the way it is. You must agree at least to work on changing this situation, or . . . (something drastic will happen. Maybe "I won't speak to you any more," or "There will be no more sex," or "Our relationship is over.") The idea here is that the partner must shape up *or else!*

Be absolutely sure you're ready to take the risk of ending the relationship before choosing this step. Most issues of the type we've been discussing aren't life-threatening or of moral importance to the degree that a radical step is worth it. But a few are (battering and alcoholism come to mind immediately). Take your time, thinking carefully about all the alternatives — and the consequences — before making a major declaration. Re-read Chapter Five on Commitment — particularly the section on "When to Say 'When'." Answer the questions in the "Knowing When to Quit Index" in Jack Barranger's book (see Bibliography).

Don't offer an ultimatum unless you're prepared to follow through on the consequences you threaten; ultimatums are only powerful if you back them up fully. And you'll need to be prepared to stick to your ultimatum until you're certain that the changes will actually solve the issue to your satisfaction — or that there really is no hope. Ending the relationship is sometimes the best solution. Are you willing to risk that?

• *Get professional help.* You'll find some guidelines for finding good professional help on pages 189-192.

On Becoming Intimate Individuals

"Individual differences" is an idea which is taken for granted in a society which calls its political freedoms "inalienable rights." But how does the idea of personal freedom work when the *person* is half of an intimate *couple*? What opportunities are there for individuality and self-expression in day-to-day relationships with someone you can reach out and touch without picking up the phone?

The boundaries of individual rights are tough enough to define in the larger community: Do we both have a "right" to that parking space we reached at the same moment? The difficulty is compounded at home: Do I have a "right" to invite a bunch of friends over to watch "Monday Night Football" without consulting my mate? If so, have I shown adequate respect for her? My partner surely has a "right" to ridicule my first attempt at watercolor painting, but I'll be devastated nonetheless.

Hair styles, clothing, favorite TV shows, hobbies, accents, political or religious beliefs, career choices, pets, music — there are a thousand ways each of us can demonstrate our individuality. Let's celebrate the freedom we enjoy which makes it possible — and let's cherish the intimate partners who support and encourage us in our self-expression.

Intimacy is more satisfying, joyous, and alive when the individuality of each partner is honored. Remember, there are two "me's" in a healthy "we."

intimate environments

No Relationship Is An Island

Over the last three decades, we've all become more aware of the high level of interdependence among the elements of the Earth's ecosystem. A volcanic eruption in Washington state affects the weather in Central America. A nuclear plant accident in the Soviet Union kills reindeer in Iceland. Heavy beef consumption in the United States accelerates the destruction of the rain forests in Central and South America.

It's like that on a small scale also. Every living organism is subject to an array of forces from inside and outside itself. Some forces are destructive, some are nurturing, and some can be both (such as heat, which is necessary and healthy in some measure — and can destroy if elevated beyond a critical point).

Thus far in this book our focus has been on the six major dimensions *within* your intimate relationship. But many factors influence an intimate organism from *outside* as well, and at times, these may be even more influential:

Human Environment (People, relationships)
Economic Environment (Employment, financial resources)
Natural Environment (Geographic setting, weather)
Built Environment (Home, workplace, community structures)
Lifestyle Environment (Time, religion, food, health, media, leisure)
Sociocultural Environment (Ethnic community, mores, values)
Political Environment (Government influence, freedom)

You'll recall in Chapter 2 we pictured the intimate relationship in a sea of environmental forces, something like this:

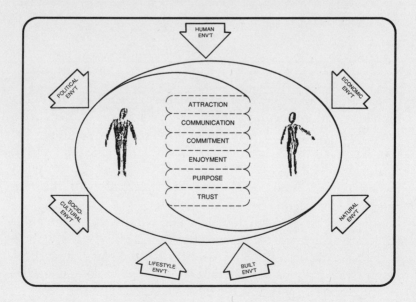

We can't cover in detail every environmental factor which influences a relationship, of course (and you wouldn't want us to — some of this stuff is pretty boring!). Still, these are very important pressures on our intimate partnerships, and we must not overlook them, or minimize their importance. Let's take a look at how environments are significant to intimacy.

How Does the Environment Influence a Relationship?

Much is known about the effects of the environment on human individuals and groups from studies in environmental psychology, social psychology, ethology, family systems, and the biology of organisms. Here are a few key facts:

• Sometimes the environment is *nurturing* toward the organism (e.g. the loving support of friends and family in a crisis), and sometimes it is *destructive* (e.g. loss of a job).

• The effect of any outside factor depends upon your *perception and interpretation* of it (*how you see* job pressures on your relationship is more important than how they really are).

• The influence of an environmental factor depends upon the *strength of your connection to it* (you are likely to be affected more by immediate family members than by acquaintances).

• The influence of an environmental factor depends in part on *your early experiences with it* and your early learning about it.

• Organisms have remarkable *capacities to adapt* to their environments, although such "adaptation" is not always healthy.

• An organism will — in general — *try to maintain its internal state* despite extreme variations in its environment.

• Humans are among the very few organisms which have significant capacities to *modify their environments* at will.

• Organisms *become more cohesive* when they must deal with disruptions or threats from any source in the external environment.

Response to your environment is an area in which you and your partner have an opportunity to express your individual and joint uniqueness. Microbiologist Rene Dubos observed that "each organism has its own peculiar way of responding to the total environment." (And everybody knows just how peculiar some folks can be . . . .)

The rest of this chapter examines each of the major environmental influences on the intimate organism.

Human Environment

The other people in your life are your most obvious and influential environmental factors. Children, parents, brothers and sisters, cousins, aunts and uncles, all manner of other relatives, friends, neighbors, co-workers, bosses . . . Everybody wants a piece of your life. Their pressure for your time and attention can place major strains on your intimate partnership. And their nurturing can be of immeasurable value.

You have something to gain from each of these relationships, yet they all demand time and energy. They can make it more difficult at times when you need privacy and time alone together. And they can help by supporting you in times of need, from a simple babysitting arrangement that lets you get away from your little ones for a few hours, to an understanding shoulder to cry on when things have gone awry.

Clearly children are the most powerful "external" influence on the intimate relationship (when there are children) partly because they're so close. They're barely external at all. They must have your attention — indeed, when they're very young they can't survive without it — but you also must make time for yourselves. The balancing act necessary can be very demanding.

Ideas about dress, behavior, music, child rearing, TV, values, politics, money . . . virtually everything, change with each generation. Parents of both partners in an intimate relationship are bound to be influential — in the early years because it's hard for them to let go of you, and later because they may need your assistance. We all start out, of course, as products of our early experiences with our "families of origin."

Do you live with your parents or in-laws? Their influence will be even more powerful under those circumstances. Such an arrangement was traditional in extended families — particularly among some cultural groups — in previous generations. After World War II, it became customary in the United States for young marrieds to make separate homes on their own. In very recent years, however, the extremely high cost of housing has led many young couples to reconsider their needs for "privacy and independence," In increasing numbers, young couples are reportedly finding ways to expand the parental homestead so they can "come back home." Such arrangements have very powerful effects on the intimate relationship, and must be considered with great care so that the economic, space, social and emotional needs of both partners and the host family are dealt with as fairly as possible. TV's most popular program of the mid 1970s — *All in the Family* — taught us much about the tricky balancing act involved when everybody is under one roof.

Your family's communication styles may not be yours. Family presence can stifle intimate communication. Yet, other family members may provide models of openness and in other ways stimulate you to deal with festering issues.

You and your partner may, like most folks, have a sense of obligation to your families. But your families may carry that too far, and think they should still come first. On the other hand, your family may be an important source of support for your commitment to each other, since family members may offer encouragement for staying together when you may want to part.

Friends and neighbors, like family, can be great sources of support and nurturance, and can create significant time and energy demands on a couple. Friends who are needy, perhaps with emotional or financial difficulties, may begin to interfere with your intimacy by their requests for your help. And friends of one partner aren't always favorites with the other partner — that can create special problems for the relationship.

Large families can provide lots of activities and fun. But family activities can get in the way of your own. Balance — in favor of your relationship — is recommended.

Family values can instill a sense of purpose. But your purpose as a couple may conflict with family ideas. Once you're on your own, it's important to follow the path you and your partner map out. Don't turn your back on all you've grown up with, however. Just use it as a foundation, not as a ceiling.

Your family may not approve of your lifestyle, of course. But you must decide for yourselves how you'll live. Don't waste energy reacting against the lifestyle of your family, though. "Decide for yourselves" means neither *because* of them nor *in spite* of them; it means *without* them.

Close involvement with families can raise issues of trust: "Will you tell the family our secrets?" "Can I trust your family?" "Why don't you trust my family?" Keep your communication tools sharp!

Friends and neighbors are an important part of your interpersonal support network. You need them, and they need you, particularly in times of difficulty. Make room for them in your life.

Suggestions:

• Establish your intimate organism as your first priority whenever possible.

• Allow time and energy to meet your children's needs when they're very young and can't provide for themselves, BUT remember to . . .

• View child rearing as a process of helping them become independent adults who do not need your help.

• Let family members and friends know, by your actions and your words, that your relationship comes first for you. But treat them with consideration and respect.

• Learn how to say "no" before other people become a burden to your relationship.

- Take intiative when you can to maintain relationships with other people. Don't cut yourselves off in your zeal to nurture your intimacy.

Economic Environment

Economic 1: Employment — The pressures of the workplace — especially in a time when the economics of mere survival are so difficult — create particularly difficult burdens for intimacy. In most intimate partnerships these days, both partners are working out of pure economic necessity.

In the beginning, they may have found each other because they work together, or because he admired her professional achievements, or she his creativity. No matter. Sooner or later their jobs will be the source of some trouble as they fight to maintain a sense of intimacy in the face of business travel, layoffs, unequal pay for equal work, "homework," evening meetings, too-much-month-left-at-the-end-of-the-money, and other pressures related to work.

Employment can be an extremely powerful environmental influence on the intimate organism. Absence of a stable source of economic support can easily destroy a loving relationship; not because it leads lovers to care less for one another (indeed, such adversity can pull them together), but because the economic and psychological needs for such endeavors are so fundamental that self-respect becomes very vulnerable. ("I can't get a job; I'm worthless; she'd be better off without me . . ..") Such situations demand extreme sensitivity — and strong commitment on the part of intimate partners.

Employment is often a very positive force in loving relationships, of course. People with similar career and educational backgrounds tend to be attracted to one another. Those with better jobs and educations also are attractive to others who are trying to improve their situations in life.

Similar educational levels generally enhance communication, and common career interests can provide ongoing topics for conversation. (But such a basis for connection can get in the way of *intimate* communication, since the talk may focus on business, rather than relationship!)

Commitment may be enhanced while a couple works toward educational or career goals, but may be inhibited by achieving those goals. Glenda, for example, worked as a nurse to put Aaron through medical school. The ink was barely dry on his diploma when Aaron filed for divorce.

Later in life, security issues loom large, along with inertia, and the couple may stay together because it's the easiest thing to do.

Common interests can enhance enjoyment, but job interests don't necessarily mean fun! Similar educational levels may lead to similar leisure interests (e.g., tennis is more likely to go with a college background; bowling has traditionally been a blue-collar sport).

"Improve your status" is a major component of the Great American Dream. A better education and a better job often give purpose and direction to a relationship in the early years.

If there is a big discrepancy in your educations, there may be some tendency to distrust ("Will you prefer somebody else — somebody more educated?")

Suggestions

• Set your individual priorities on job and career issues, then work cooperatively to reach common goals.

• Don't pretend there's no problem. Recognize that competition of energies and loyalties will always create some level of difficulty. Develop ways, including regular discussion and negotiation, to deal with the problem so it doesn't create a major obstacle to your intimacy.

• If you elect to favor relationship and family goals over career advancement, be prepared to pay a price on the job.

• If you elect to favor career goals over relationship and family, be prepared to pay a price at home.

Economic 2: Financial Resources — Like employment, the presence or absence of financial resources can be both an inhibitor and an enhancer of intimacy.

In the flush of early romance, lovers don't really care much about money. They figure that the money will come and circumstances will get better. And, for most folks, they do. But intimacy may never be better than when you have little in the way of material substance.

Stereotypically, folks with more money are more attractive. Money isn't a very idealistic reason to be attracted to someone, but it's an undeniable force. Similarity is another big force, however, and a major gap in socioeconomic levels can be a big barrier to the development of a strong intimate partnership.

Lack of money can create real communication problems in a relationship, especially if basic survival needs are threatened, or if one partner thinks the other isn't pulling a fair share of the load. Surprisingly, couples who *have* a lot of money say it can create problems if partners disagree on what to do with it, how it will be handled or by whom . . . Communication about financial matters, and shared responsibility for money decisions, are among the most common problem areas in marriages. Again, maybe not the best of reasons, but money does become a factor in whether couples stay together. She may stay because he has it; he may leave because she doesn't.

Money can enhance leisure opportunities; some activities are impossible without it. But time is equally important, and often making money takes the time away from fun. Workaholics can forget how to have fun, or get so "busy" they don't allow themselves time.

Money can be a purpose of its own, but it's a pretty weak one. Not because it's "the root of all evil," but because it's elusive (subject to many factors beyond your control), and illusive (having it seems more important when you don't than when you do — there's never "enough.") Better: see it as a means to better ends: a better life for your intimate partnership and your family, support for causes you believe in, a way to help create a better world . . .

Money raises inevitable issues of trust — perhaps more than any element of the relationship other than sex. Can I trust you with the money? Will you pay the bills on time? Will you gamble, drink it away? Will you shop wisely for groceries, clothes, household needs?

Suggestions:

• Make sure your money works for you by investing wisely. (Does your checking account pay interest?)

• Borrow only when you *really* need to. The days of "maximum debt" as a good idea — if they ever existed — are dead in the current economy. Cash rules! (Careless debt is one of the greatest pressures on relationships. Don't buy that extra car or boat or bedroom set until you have *at least* half the money in hand.)

• When you must borrow, shop carefully for credit terms. The money business is as competitive as the auto business; you *can* negotiate!

• Let money serve your other priorities — don't let it become one.

• You'll have to work hard to get it, but don't get caught in the trap of letting the pursuit become the goal.

• Set your priorities and stick with them.

• Keep your expenditures in balance. If there is money for his new weight machine, there is money for her new cross-country skis.

Built Environment

"The built environment" is a term architects, planners, and environmental psychologists use for the buildings and developed spaces we live in and around. If you live in a city, you have a more fully developed "built environment" than your cousins in rural communities.

A few observations:

It's harder to stay attractive if you don't have indoor plumbing.

Communication is inhibited by paper-thin walls or a too-small house. Lack of room for everybody means the children will likely interfere with intimate communication.

Maybe the cost of housing keeps you together. It's tougher than ever to afford to live alone. That's not a good reason, but if it is reality for you, perhaps you can find a way to make it more comfortable by working at your intimate relationship, using some of the procedures outlined in this book.

Physical space can make a lot of difference in your enjoyment of life. A recent program by the city of Chicago to clean up crime and drugs in public housing complexes has resulted in improved attitudes and community pride among the people who live there.

If you're fortunate, your home may provide room for hobbies, space for a garden, art and music if you like it, books, a view, access to amenities, good schools. Your quality of life is much enhanced by your living space — if it's good space.

Architects and space planners have identified helpful tools for visualizing the "situational context" of a relationship. Key factors in such an analysis include physical boundaries of place, space between people and objects, temperature, light, noise, odor, colors, humidity. Are the individuals and the partnership compatible with the space? These factors will help you to understand how *your* space measures up.

Here are a few of the adjectives commonly used to describe space (which apply to yours?): pleasing, arousing, peaceful, hectic, festive, disgusting, boring, joyful, inspiring, alive, inviting, depressing, fresh, relaxing, cool, warm, natural, high-tech.

Some studies have shown that environmental factors are more important as a relationship develops than they are at first. In the beginning, the individuals are so focused on the personal and interpersonal variables that the setting is relatively unimportant. As the relationship grows more intimate, environmental factors become more noticeable. How come? Probably because in the early days we're "blinded by love," and later we're more aware of reality.

Environmental variables change with your age, too. For teens, noise appears to be a plus. Youngsters want lots of action, sights and sounds, stimulation which matches their internal energy level. Older adults, on the other hand, have very different needs, in sync with their slower emotional and physical pace.

Another interesting research result: there are significant differences in satisfaction with an environment among people of different ages, ethnic groups, socioeconomic and marital status. You may find the house which you love today not at all suitable ten years hence, or if you divorce, or if your income jumps (or falls).

Cultural and lifestyle choices are stronger predictors of home environment differences than are such physical conditions as safety, repair condition, cleanliness, orderliness, visual factors, according to studies by environmental researchers.

Suggestions:
 • If your home and budget allow for it, or if you're planning a new home, consider providing different types of environmental areas, including individual spaces (for privacy and special interests), public spaces (for greeting and entertaining others), shared spaces (bathrooms, utility areas), jurisdictional spaces (for special use by "in charge" family member — e.g. kitchen, shop), activity spaces (for family activities).
 • Plan *together* for design, decoration, and use of spaces in the home.
 • Don't burden yourselves with more home than you can afford — in expenses, in energy, in time.
 • Remember that your home needs change with time. And neighborhoods change. Be flexible enough to modify your

home, or even to move if need be, to meet your changing partnership and/or family needs.

Natural Environment

Most inhabited areas of the United States started out as beautiful natural environments. Native Americans accepted the environment as they found it, considered it a blessing — however bleak it may appear to us today — and learned to live in cooperation with it. Later immigrants decided they could improve upon nature. They built near natural sources of water, with other abundant natural resources nearby (because they didn't yet have the means to transport them from elsewhere). Gradually at first, then rapidly, they used up those resources and had to create the technology to import them.

Meanwhile, inhabited areas became more crowded, and people became more dependent on imported resources, and less on their own survival skills. In the course of these developments, much of the natural environmental beauty which attracted them in the first place disappeared. The "natural" environment became harder to find, and they had to travel away from home to appreciate it.

Relationships which are nurtured in non-natural environments — primarily human-built spaces — must deal with the additional burden of not having beautiful sunsets (or sunrises), not hearing the sounds of natural waterways, not sharing their life spaces with other species . . .

Do you and your partner need "natural" space? Do you prefer the excitement and pace of the city? Have you considered together such issues as aesthetics, pollution, availability of water, crowding, loneliness, climate, pollution, scenery, air, water . . . and how they affect your relationship?

Suggestions:
* Look for opportunities to spend time in other environ-

ments. If you're going to go back to school, for example, consider going to an entirely new and different locale.

• Find out as much as you can about your own natural surroundings. Take hikes and nature walks. Visit museums. Get a telescope and view the stars. Go to lecture-slide shows.

• Travel together. (This can have remarkable effects on other aspects of your intimacy as well. Carl and Nancy had tried for years to have a child; they went to Europe for a summer and, voila! Pregnant.)

• Work to improve your environment. Join a community action group to start recycling waste. Tell city hall you want more street trees.

• Add natural landscape materials to your own immediate living environment. Plant trees, or buy indoor plants. (Be sure to pay attention to drought or other conditions which may suggest particular varieties.)

Lifestyle Environment

Lifestyle 1: Time — Do you feel you have enough time for everything in your life? Does anybody? Time is the ultimate determinant of our experiences. Despite our fervent wishes, we're given only 24 hours in a day, 7 days in a week, 52 weeks in a year, and (for nearly everybody) something less than 100 years in a lifetime.

When is there time to work at remaining *attractive*? Who has time to *communicate* clearly enough and often enough? *Commitment* means — more or less — a lifetime. But some folks feel they must take full advantage of every opportunity to "have new experiences" which may interfere with commitment.

Enjoyment is more a state of mind than anything else. But if you think in terms of partying, or vacations, or recreational activities, time is the great obstacle. And the "when-I's" may be the greatest robber of enjoyment known to humankind. Instead of enjoying life as it is lived, ambitious folks are wont to postpone enjoyment — "when I . . . " (finish a project, graduate from school, move, get my house, pay off my car, get that promotion, get the children through school, get the mortgage paid off, win the lottery.) Each promise puts off enjoyment till "later." So when is "later"?

How you use your time, of course, is the greatest single measure of your *purpose* in life. Ben Franklin advised: "Dost thou love life? Then do not squander time, for that's the stuff life is made of."

Time has another important influence on relationships. "Can I *trust* you to be there when I need you?" "Will you still love me when I'm 64?"

A recent study of "circadian rhythms" — the internal biological clocks by which we all function — suggests that many couples are "asynchronous." Their sleep/wake cycles are mismatched. Of the 150 or so couples involved in the study reported in *Psychology Today*, 82 had different time cycles. The most important result: 32% of the time-mismatched couples had "troubled marriages," while only 8% of cycle-matched pairs did. The researchers acknowledge that cause and effect aren't demonstrated by these data. It may be that their sleep cycles are messed up by a troubled marriage. Whichever way the clock runs, however, such differences require patient negotiation, and considerable creativity and flexibility to maintain harmony in the relationship. All these issues of time have critical effects on the quality of your relationship with each other and with the world. Careful management of your time and your priorities may be the greatest single investment you can make in the future of your relationship.

Suggestions:
- Make time management a clear priority. If you manage your time, it will be less likely to manage you.
- Follow Franklin's advice not to "squander" your time, but do allow time for leisure pursuits without guilt.
- You needn't live by the clock or calendar, but do keep

track of deadlines imposed by your job, your child's school, the tax man, your editor, and other forces beyond your control. Allowing yourself more time than you think you'll need to handle such events will always pay off!

• Keep your schedule "lean and mean." Unnecessary clutter is a great robber of time.

• "Quality time" with your kids is a good idea, but it's *not* a substitute for *enough* time. They need *at least* a few minutes alone with each of you every day.

• The same is true of your time for each other. Allow *at least* a half hour alone together every day.

• If there is "never time" for yourselves or your children, cut out some other activities. You cannot afford *not* to.

Lifestyle 2: Food — When you first saw this heading, perhaps you wondered, "What does food have to do with intimacy?" Much more than you might have guessed. The implications of our three-times-a-day survival and pleasure pastime are significant, indeed.

Consider the time and energy we and our neighbors put into thinking about food, planning meals, finding and/or growing and/or purchasing foods, preparing meals, eating, cleaning up after meals, going out to eat . . . .

Consider the ways food influences relationships directly: romantic candlelit dinners, picnics, champagne brunches, church socials, singles progressive dinners, quick lunches in the automat or at McDonalds, coffee breaks, inviting a special person over to dinner, "staying for breakfast." Or, for some folks, sharing the last scraps at the homeless shelter, going hungry, asking for handouts, collecting scraps at the back doors of restaurants. Food is truly a universal life force.One unfortunate side effect of the emphasis on healthy foods in recent years has been that many people have mistakenly believed that healthy food is automatically expensive. Not true. White bread, fried foods, high-sugar and high cholesterol snacks, high-calorie sodas, canned vegetables and other poor nuturition foods are generally *more* expensive than their healthy counterparts. Lots of folks simply aren't informed, or don't bother to comparison shop for healthier products.

Even though, alas, there are no proven "aphrodisiacs," many other effects of nutrition on health and vitality are well documented. You don't have to start visiting "health food" stores, but you should be looking at your own diet and its contribution to your physical and emotional well-being. Not only can you improve your energy levels and sense of health, you might just live longer!

Suggestions:

• Learn all you can about good nutrition, but be careful about exotic dietary supplements and other substances which make exaggerated claims. Careful scientific research has consistently shown that we all need a good balanced diet (that *doesn't* mean the "four food groups" they taught you in school!): low in saturated fat (note that all fat isn't saturated), high in dietary fiber (note that all "fiber" isn't dietary), and low in salt.

• Try to use food creatively. Try new things. (Your partner might rave about a new recipe you prepare with tofu — especially if the key ingredient isn't announced in advance!

• Use foods which are as fresh as possible. Lots of folks who claim not to like fish find it very appealing when they finally experience it *fresh* from the ocean, lake, or stream. Similarly with fresh vegetables.

• *Never, never* put salt on or in food without tasting it first. Americans and some Europeans use *much* more salt than is necessary or healthy — and often *cover* the taste of good food in the process.

Lifestyle 3: Media — "Where'd you get that idea?" Well, if you're like most of us, chances are pretty good "that idea" came from TV, or a magazine, or radio, or the movies, or a popular song . . . We're influenced by the media more than we know, and more — much more — than we like to admit.

Much of our thinking about intimate relationships comes from TV sitcoms, romantic movies, and love songs (of whatever musical genre).

The media exert—directly and indirectly—a tremendously powerful influence on the intimate organism and the individual partners. The very stuff of TV and movies includes models of "ideal" relationships, how to talk to each other, how to dress, moral values, child rearing, drugs, alcohol, sex, violence, what's important in the larger community and world . . .

What's more, we spend a tremendous amount of time being entertained by the media.

Suggestions:

• Make conscious and informed choices about your media exposure and that of your children — don't just accept what the networks throw at us.

• Question the values represented by programming.

• Remember TV and movie fiction represents a fantasy world. The actors always know exactly what to say —like former President Ronald Reagan — because somebody else wrote it for them! You and I — and our love partners — don't have the luxury of script writers; we have to wing it minute by minute.

• Let yourself watch, listen to, and read about new ideas, and viewpoints you disagree with.

• Ask yourself — when you're being critical of your partner's appearance, or attitudes, or style — if you are using a TV or movie (fantasy world) model as a standard of comparison. Remember how unrealistic that is.

Lifestyle 4: Religion/Values — We know, we know. You're *not* "religious," so this part doesn't apply to you.

Guess again. It's virtually impossible to live in Western

society and not be influenced by organized religion and/or the values it represents.

Although differentness can be appealing too, we're most often attracted to someone who shares our religious ideas. Religion may be an area of communication between partners even if they profess none, since such issues as abortion, child rearing, capital punishment, social justice and equality of the sexes are associated with religious viewpoints.

Religion is a very demanding commitment of its own, and if it's shared, the couple has a strong external bond. If it's not shared, the seed is planted for possibly painful hours as the religious traditions of the partners are exercised.

Church activities, when willingly shared by the partners, can be a source of leisure fun. Strong shared values can enhance enjoyment in the relationship.

Shared religious commitment offers a very strong foundation for a sense of "higher purpose" in a relationship. And mutual commitment to a spiritual/religious ideal can make partners appear more trustworthy to each other. Generally, religious ideals can enhance trust, but there are no guarantees that religious partners won't hurt each other.

Non-religious values are just as important as those fostered by religious organizations. You may believe in humanistic values, including the ultimate perfectibility of each human being. Or perhaps concern for world peace or the environment is at the top of your priorities.

Your values determine your attitudes toward other people, the political system, and your daily experiences. They shape much of your use of your time, energy, and money. Whatever your personal value system, it will be a major force in shaping your intimate relationship.

Suggestions:
  • Put some time and energy into clarifying your own personal value system — religious or otherwise.

• Be sure your partner understands your values and priorities *early* in the relationship. They will affect your partnership in powerful ways — positive or destructive.

• Work with your partner to develop as many *shared* values as you can. They will form a strong foundation for a lasting intimate partnership.

• Recognize that values are subject to change over time. You may experience a religious conversion, or discover a new aspect of life, or find yourself committed to a political, social, economic, environmental, or other cause. Any such life-changing experience can have major effects on your value system.

• Live your values, and make room for your partner to do so as well.

Sociocultural Environment

Sociocultural 1: Social Roles — Who are you? Well, you're a lot of folks in a single package. You see yourself in a particular way (better than anybody else, but not very objectively), your partner sees a slightly different you, as do your parents, children, siblings, neighbors, co-workers, boss, volunteer group committee members, church cohorts, dentist, and others.

The various social roles we play — not as if on stage, but roles nonetheless — can have a major impact on intimate relationships. If you don't effectively handle a problem with neighbors, you may lose something in your partner's eyes. If you keep your cool in a disagreement with the Little League umpire, your young ballplayer will regard you as an even more special hero(ine).

Other social roles which play a part in your interaction with the community include your socioeconomic position (others have expectations of you which depend on your perceived ability to contribute), volunteer roles you have assumed (managing the school carnival is a time-and-energy-demanding task), parenting responsibilities, care of aging parents, visibility (very private persons have fewer social expectation pressures from outside).

Suggestions:
- Move slowly in this arena. You'll find people will be anxious to embrace you as a new "volunteer" if you express interest in a community program. Be sure you're ready before you make yourself available.
- Find out as much as you can about community activities before you sign on. How much time is expected — really? Does membership require financial support? Does the organization get involved in politics, and if so, do their politics agree with yours? Are the leaders and active members people you respect? Do they welcome new members for their financial and energy contributions, but never let them into the "inner circle"?

Sociocultural 2: Culture — This is an almost hidden, yet very powerful, element of the environment. Consider the amazing differences in attitudes about relationships among such varied cultural groups as Native Americans, African Americans, Northern European Americans, Asian Americans — attitudes about living together before marriage, number of children, living close to families of origin, intercultural marriage, maintaining cultural traditions . . .

Typical issues: Is divorce okay? How many children shall we have? May we live anywhere we want, or must we stay near family? In what group/community activities shall we participate? What jobs are okay for a woman who works outside the home? What jobs are okay for a man who works outside the home?

Suggestions:
- Don't try to deny your cultural heritage.
- If your partner comes from another cultural background,

see if you can find ways to celebrate both cultures creatively (your children will inherit both).

• Look for ways your culture contributes to growth of your intimate organism.

Sociocultural 3: Discrimination — One of the most destructive forces in society is the denial of fair treatment because of race, age, sex, religion, or other irrelevant factors.

Discrimination, whatever the basis, is an insidious evil which poisons both the victim and the perpetrator. Intimate relationships which must deal with racism, sexism, and the like are drained of energy and vitality which might otherwise help to build a stronger intimate organism (which in turn could give back much to the larger community).

The decade of the 1980s saw in the United States drastic cutbacks in public support for key social programs. It is evident that many of those steps, while taken ostensibly for economic reasons (there really isn't enough money to do everything), were directed against the politically powerless: the poor, minorities, elderly. Pressure placed on families by reductions in welfare support are often noted as the cause of breakups of intimate relationships. Although there have been a few positive reforms in the welfare system, one intimacy-destroying policy is still in effect in many areas: a woman can often get more money from public assistance as a single parent than she and her husband could earn together.

Discrimination also leads to related environmental problems. Slum landlords may allow buildings to deteriorate, using as their excuse the racist notion that "minority tenants won't take care of property anyway." Politicians select communities without political power for unpopular projects: prisons, waste dumps, industrial zones. Rev. Jesse Jackson recently observed that "Toxic waste is not deposited in Beverly Hills or Chevy Chase. It is stowed away in the middle of the night in poor communities in places like Arkansas, Louisiana and South Carolina."

There are no simple answers to problems of discrimination. As soon as an antidiscriminatory policy is made law, bigots find ways to circumvent it, or to discriminate in other ways. Minority children are taunted by their peers; there is no law that prevents kids from being psychologically cruel to one another. Mixed-race couples often are denied acceptance in both ethnic communities; the law doesn't prevent us from disowning our children if they don't do things our way. Religious communities appear to give comfort and sanctuary, but many churches are strongholds of racism and intolerance.

These issues must be addressed on a larger societal scale. For the individual couple it means seeking environments in which their relationship can grow stronger, and in which they can raise families without fear. Such places are tough to find, and tough to keep.

For more than two decades, we have advocated outspoken personal assertiveness as one method for dealing with intolerable circumstances. In our book, *Your Perfect Right*, we note,

"It is our hope that more adequately assertive expression will preclude the necessity of aggression among the activist politically alienated. The growth and successes of assertive citizen lobbies, — the civil rights movement, . . . the Grey Panthers, . . . — are powerful evidence: assertion does work! And there may be no more important arena for its application than overcoming the sense of 'What's the use? I can't make a difference,' that tends to pervade the realm of personal political action."

Discriminatory environments can hurt — or even destroy — an intimate organism. But they can also be sources of strength. Use the common enemy as a basis for pooling your resources and your talents. Let the pressures from outside make you more cohesive, and enhance your determination to help your own relationship grow and thrive.

The problems are real, and they won't go away anytime soon. The obstacles are difficult, but not insurmountable. Meanwhile, you may find some solace in the pseudo-Latin slogan, *Non illegitimus carborundum.* (Don't let the bastards grind you down!)

Suggestions

• Know your rights. Get familiar with federal, state, and local laws which prohibit discrimination. Information is your best resource in this field.

• Stay in touch. Know your neighbors, and talk openly with them about problems of discrimination, individual or institutional.

• Use groups effectively. Churches, parent-teacher groups, community organizations — even national societies — are powerful allies, and you're battling a powerful enemy.

• Use the media when appropriate. Particularly in political situations, the media can take on the "powers that be" more effectively than you can begin to alone.

• Keep your priorities straight. Make sure your own personal goals are being served by your activities. Don't become the scapegoat or sacrificial lamb for someone else's cause, unless it's also *your* cause.

• Remember your intimate partnership and your family. If you publicly take on issues of discrimination, you may help make a better world for everyone. You may also expose your family to some tough times. Include them in the decision, and monitor the effects on them as you go.

• Read. Lots of folks have written well about their experiences battling this most pernicious of human evils. Do your homework, and don't waste energy reinventing wheels.

Political Environment

Applied for a building permit recently? Tried to cut down those street trees that are tearing up your driveway? Satisfied with your garbage collection service? How do you feel about bailing out the savings and loan industry at a personal cost of more than $1000 a year? Does the federal government's priority of $1,000,000 on weapons for every $1 on education agree with your priorities?

The political environment may affect us only indirectly (such as how many unrelated people can live in the house down the block), or it may press on our daily lives (such as how much we pay in taxes to support government activities), but it's surely going to be a source of some stress — and at times some support — for our relationships. Taxes and other policies with which we disagree are likely to upset our relationships to the degree that the individual partners are upset by them. Meanwhile, government efforts to make neighborhoods safer and schools more effective may enhance our quality of life, and hence our intimacy.

The social, political, economic, geographic environment in which you live can have major effects on your intimate organism. Rural or urban, high-rise or acreage, booming or dying, high-employment or poverty, good public services or a decaying infrastructure — all can have significant effects on your relationship.

Suggestions
• Remember that politics changes with time — and the tenure of politicians. As the Texas rancher says about the local weather: "If you don't like it, stick around for a while."
• Allow three times as long as you believe it should take for any project which requires local government approval.
• Take a few minutes to call or write your elected representatives about issues which concern you. You may be surprised at how responsive they are, especially at the local level.
• If you and your partner disagree on political issues, you're not alone! Try *really listening* to each other's views on a regular basis. Give each other copies of thoughtful articles

presenting your view. *Read* articles representing his/her view. Remember that the democratic political system works because reasonable people are willing to negotiate and compromise; you can too.

No Relationship Is An Island

The environment in which your intimate organism lives is a key element in determining the quality and health of your relationship. Environmental forces become a part of the *system*, acting on your intimate organism and reacting to it. Although many of these factors appear on the surface to be out of control, you can have something to say about the environment in which you and your partner live. As we have discussed in this chapter, you can take assertive action to make your intimate environment a largely positive force in the health of your intimate organism.

Since it's going to be a part of the *system* anyway, why not make the environment a part of your *team*?

nurturing your intimate organism

Taking Care of Caring (and Getting Help When You Need It)

There you have it.

We've presented a six-dimensional model for your intimate relationship, discussed how the dimensions work together, and added some perspective on the environment in which the "intimate organism" lives. Now it's your turn. What will you do with this information? Will you use it to help your intimate partnership grow and prosper?

In each chapter of this book, we've offered practical suggestions designed to help you make your own relationship better and more fulfilling for you and your partner. How you apply — or ignore — these ideas is, of course, up to you. Every relationship is unique, and everyone's needs are different. We do hope you'll not simply stick the book on a shelf and return to business as usual. Surely your relationship deserves better.

This "wrap-up" chapter adds a few ideas about making it all work — implementing the suggestions we've presented earlier, *nurturing* your own intimate organism, and finding competent professional guidance when you need it.

On the Nature of Nurture

Who — or what — have you nurtured lately? Have you been kind to someone who was ill? Was a houseplant rootbound and looking a bit sickly? Did your dog, horse, cat, or parakeet need some care? Perhaps one of your children wanted some quality attention, or maybe you were around a tiny baby and gave some nurturance. How about your intimate partner, yourself, your relationship, or other parts of your intimate organism?

The nourishment you give in these situations runs a wide gamut. Empathetic listening, providing a bigger pot for a plant, feeding a pet, giving a child a bath or a few dollars to spend, cooing to a baby — all are viable ways to be a good nurturer. And, lest you think that nurturing is always a pleasant task, there may be times of gentle confrontation: challenging an inconsistency, administering discipline, admonishing one to do better. Or you may "nurture" by doing the dishes when it's not your turn, helping with yardwork, changing a messy diaper, or repairing the broken gate latch. The many ways of nurturing are always caring, but not necessarily things you will relish doing!

Dictionaries speak of *nurturance* as "affectionate care and attention," and of *nurture* as "something that nourishes." Applied to the intimate organism, nurturance means both partners nourish and support each other, themselves, and the partnership, so that the organism grows and stays healthy. When you share in the special task of developing yourselves and your partnership, you help build a stronger family, *and* benefit the larger community. Don't forget the quality which is the foundation for it all: *ACCEPTance.* Fully accepting yourself as you are, and similarly accepting your partner, with all his or her strengths and shortcomings, may be the most nurturing step you can take. On the surface, acceptance appears to be a passive action. Don't be fooled. It demands your best and most active energy: compassion, understanding, empathy, forgiveness, support, love, belief, openness, affirmation.

Nurturing means taking a step out of a miserly, encapsulated, self-engrossed attitude into an attitude of giving generated from the heart. The nurturing attitude is a soft, loving approach to ourselves and others. Set aside your daily worries and step out of yourself; be kinder to yourself, your partner, and others. It requires a conscious effort, a caring response, perhaps a risk.

"Okay, Okay ... I Get The Point! But What Do l Do? "

There's no limit to the ways you can nurture yourself, your partner, and your intimate organism. One way to start is with the six dimensions: attraction, commitment, communication, enjoyment, purpose, and trust. The starter lists on the following pages will help you generate your own set of ways to nurture your relationship, based on the six dimensions. These are only a small suggestion of possible ways to nurture. The "enjoyment" dimension alone could be tapped for thousands of ideas! Each intimate organism is unique, and the list of ways to nurture it is boundless. Fill up a journal page with your own ideas for each dimension.

ATTRACTION

Yourself: Treat yourself to a new article of clothing.

_____

_____

_____

Partner: Compliment your partner on looking good.

_____

_____

_____

Relationship: Jointly agree on a project to make the house more attractive.

_____

_____

_____

Environment: Pay special attention to one of your relatives.

_____

_____

_____

_____

_____

_____

_____

_____

_____

_____

_____

_____

_____

COMMUNICATION

Yourself: Catch your train of negative thoughts before it runs you down.

_____
_____
_____

Partner: Speak to your partner about a negative behavior you've noticed recently.

_____
_____
_____

Relationship: Discuss how you two can make your relationship more open and spontaneous.

_____
_____
_____

Environment: Decide to be more friendly with your co-workers.

_____
_____
_____
_____
_____
_____
_____
_____
_____
_____
_____

COMMITMENT

Yourself: Use will power to finish a project you've put off.

_____

_____

_____

Partner: Affirm that you're committed to helping her or him achieve a special goal.

_____

_____

_____

Relationship: Commit yourselves to being firmer with the children.

_____

_____

_____

Environment: Join an organization whose values you can dedicate yourself to.

_____

_____

_____

_____

_____

_____

_____

_____

_____

_____

_____

_____

_____

ENJOYMENT

Yourself: Do something you did as a child that brought you enjoyment. Regress a little!

_____

_____

_____

Partner: Share with your partner a comic strip that would tickle him or her.

_____

_____

_____

Relationship: Plan a trip to a small town you haven't been to before. Look for unique ways to have fun.

_____

_____

_____

Environment: Have a party for the people on your block.

_____

_____

_____

_____

_____

_____

_____

_____

_____

_____

_____

_____

PURPOSE

Yourself: Set a goal for yourself to accomplish a secret desire.

_____

_____

_____

Partner: Ask your partner to tell you about any goals that you could help him or her achieve.

_____

_____

_____

Relationship: Decide together on one thing you could do to strengthen the goals of your relationship.

_____

_____

_____

Environment: Work on developing a goal of giving more of your talents back to the local community.

_____

_____

_____

_____

_____

_____

_____

_____

_____

_____

_____

_____

TRUST

Yourself: Be more reliable in what you promise yourself or others you will do. Follow through more consistently.

_____

_____

_____

Partner: Do the tasks you promise you will do, in a more timely fashion.

_____

_____

_____

Relationship: Discuss trust issues in the relationship. How can you two improve?

_____

_____

_____

Environment: Work on trusting others in your outer world more. Watch your tendency to think the worst case scenario about religion, politics, education, etc.

_____

_____

_____

_____

_____

_____

_____

_____

_____

_____

Log It!

To help you generate nurturing ideas and to help you keep track of your efforts at nurturing, you might keep a "nurturing journal" for a while. Writing down ideas and insights helps key you into this very important part of intimacy. Keep the journal private. Don't waste time and energy comparing how much you do for your partner with what he or she does for you. (Such an approach would be counterproductive and not in the true spirit of nurturing.) You are not being a nurturer simply to be nurtured in return. Try to look at it as doing good for its own sake. You will likely get good in return anyway... unless you are too eager.

We've said it before, but it's worth repeating: happy couples do more pleasing, nurturing things for each other than do unhappy couples, but force won't make it happen. So, write down your creative thoughts for nurturing, but don't keep score on how the world — or your partner — responds.

Confronting the Challenge

Several of the nurturing examples above relate to what might be called, "gentle confrontation" or "challenge." Author John Powell, in his book, *Unconditional Love*, describes challenge as a loving-but-firm reminder to your partner to make changes. You're asking your partner to work on his or her limitations, to overcome fear or problem areas, to be open to new ways of doing things, to give up bad habits.

Challenging your partner is a very delicate matter. Powell stresses using it only after you've made certain that your mate knows you'll be supportive and encouraging and understanding. Your goal is to let your partner know that you have faith in her or him. Knowing that you're willing to "hang in there" too, and that you are open to changing and growing yourself, will help your partner find the motivation and courage to make progress.

Allen Ivey, a professor of counseling at the University of Massachusetts, speaks of "confrontation" in a similar vein, describing it as a way to help others look at hidden parts of themselves. One uses confrontation to help someone overcome being stuck or blocked, to look at discrepancies in his or her thinking or behaving. The issues can be simple — your partner claims to value promptness, but tends to be late for meals you prepare — or complex — your partner identifies "openness" as a valued characteristic of a relationship, but won't discuss touchy issues with you. Ivey says that we are only vaguely aware of these "hidden parts" of ourselves as being incongruent. Such fuzzy connections in one's mind can be brought into focus by a well constructed, gentle confrontation.

The phrase "gentle confrontation" is important here. Most think of challenge and confrontation as using force or negative power to make the other person "shape up" or pay attention. Not so. The real power of confrontation comes when it's gentle, loving, and *positive*. You aren't trying to upset the person, although that may be the first reaction. Your goal is to help your partner look at an issue that needs attention. You're making yourself vulnerable by doing so. Maybe that's what Ralph Waldo Emerson meant when he said, "Rings and other jewels are not gifts but apologies for gifts. The only gift is a portion of thyself."

Break the Routine

Nurturing on all levels of your intimate organism is best when it's not an established routine or pattern. Boredom sets in when your nurturing is always predictable — a kiss every night before retiring, flowers on Saturday, breakfast in bed on Sundays. Do things in creative ways. Put a bit of zing into it! Think up new, exciting ways to nurture. Put time and effort into your caring. Consistent, rock-solid nurturing of your intimate organism is necessary, but not enough. Don't let it become so predictable that it puts your loved one to sleep!

Stay Tuned for Intimate Signals

Another aspect of nurturing to consider carefully involves signals that your partner — or the intimate organism itself — sends out. When any part of your intimate organism isn't being cared for or nourished well enough, that part will give various messages or hints.

Think about yourself: When you neglect your own highest good, your mind-body-spirit begins to give off signals. You may feel down or confused, your body may be tired or in pain, you may feel a loss of purpose or commitment. Similarly, when you aren't nurturing your partner adequately, he or she may signal you — subtly or directly. Such signals can range from, "You don't rub my back any more" to "I'm thinking about getting a divorce." Or may take the form of flirting with others, not being responsive sexually, disinterest in partnership activities, extended time away from home, new hobbies or interests which don't involve you — all these and more can be signals which need your immediate attention.

Other people close to you may detect such signals even before you do. They may observe a general feeling of malaise, low energy. or boredom. You may fight more frequently or in different ways. You may not be a united front when disciplining the children any more, or the kids may start misbehaving in unique ways all of a sudden. Your environment may give you signals too. The boss may complain, or friends may say, "You aren't your old self" or "Are you getting along all right these days?" All aspects of your intimate organism are likely to respond when you aren't being attentive to nurturing needs.

An ongoing signaling system is a valuable asset in an intimate relationship — *if* you pay attention and take action. Waiting too long can be disastrous. Nurturing includes responsibility to be mindful, to monitor your intimate organism. Stay tuned! Awareness and attention to internal signals can tell you to take whatever corrective steps are needed to keep your intimate system in balance.

The signaling system doesn't only work to warn you of problems, of course. You get rewarding signals if you nurture. Good returns good. Like attracts like.

Your partner may give you more positive strokes, your kids might behave better, your boss could say, "You're doing a great job." When you're giving positive input, you're likely to experience positive feedback in return.

On Getting Professional Help

Despite your best efforts to nurture your intimate partnership, you're human like the rest of us, and things won't always go as you'd like. When two imperfect humans get together, there are bound to be ups and downs. Although this book provides a comprehensive model of intimate relationships and lots of good ideas on how to improve yours, no book alone can save a relationship in serious trouble.

Fortunately, if you are having serious trouble, there are expert professionals available (nearly everywhere) who can provide just the intervention you may need to turn your situation around for the better.

Professional people-helpers come in a variety of shapes, sizes, colors, and flavors. Finding them, evaluating them, and working with them can be a real challenge. The suggestions below will aid you in locating qualified professional help, and getting what you need from it:

• Get help early if your relationship is in trouble. Frequent fighting, infrequent "good times," absence of positive give-and-take, longing to be "free" or away from your partner are signs that it's time to ask for outside help.

• Mental health is a field with many specialties. Find someone who is expert in *your area of need*. A few generalizations:

Marriage and family therapists have graduate training (at masters and doctoral levels) in treating *systems* — how couples and families communicate, how they treat each other, how they function together.

Psychologists are doctoral-level specialists in various aspects of human behavior, often focusing on serious psychological problems of individuals. Many psychologists are also experts in relationship work. In some hospital settings, they are also permitted to prescribe drugs.

Psychiatrists are medical doctors who may combine medical and psychological procedures, usually in the treatment of more serious mental disorders. In work with individuals, they often employ medication to bring short-term relief of symptoms while therapy progresses.

Clinical social workers have masters degrees and expertise in problems of emotional adjustment of individuals, couples and families. They often have special expertise in working with community resources, such as out-patient mental health treatment and vocational rehabilitation programs.

Pastoral counselors are church-related helpers who have backgrounds in theology. Many have special training in counseling, and a few are also licensed therapists.

Be sure to ask about the training, experience, and credentials of anyone who offers professional services.

• To confuse matters further, there are a variety of theoretical approaches and procedures employed by the various professionals who conduct couples therapy. One of the great challenges for therapists and their clients is to be sure that therapeutic interventions match client needs!

One way to view the different methods of therapy is along a continuum from "active" to "passive." *Behavioral* and *family systems* therapists tend to employ such active techniques as communication exercises, interpersonal skills training, and homework. ("There's an exercise I think will help you learn some skills for dealing with that situation. I'd like you to try this . . .") *Humanistic/gestalt* and *analytic* therapists (of several types) usually take a less directive role, encouraging clients to express their own feelings freely, emphasizing insight and the self-curative powers of the human spirit. ("Mm, hmm. Tell me more about how you felt when he said that . . .")

As you might guess from reading this book, we favor the more active approaches.

When you are selecting a therapist, ask about the approach he or she prefers. (Many will answer, "I use a number of procedures, depending upon the needs of the client." That's a good *first* answer, but don't leave it at that. Ask him/her to give you some examples.)

• Stick to *licensed professionals*. Although a license is not a guarantee of competence, your chances of getting good help are much better, and you have recourse if you're not treated well.

• Selecting and working with a therapist involves a combination of objective and intuitive factors. Pick someone who has the credentials and expertise you need, and who "feels right" to work with. It will probably take a few sessions before you'll see much progress, but don't hesitate to seek another therapist if you've given the process a fair trial and don't feel any good is coming of it.

• Low cost help may be available through your local community mental health center, family services center, college counseling clinic (check with departments of psychology, education, social work), public hospital, public health department. Many communities also have services for special needs (particular illnesses, substance abuse, child guidance, . . .)

• Find out at your first visit — or even in advance — about the services and fees. Ask for a statement — written is better — which covers: qualifications of the therapist, types of therapy offered, procedures employed, expected outcomes, fees charged.

• Accept the fact that you're going to have to change something in your life if things are going to get better. Changing behavior and/or relationships is hard work, and won't happen overnight. You'll need to enter therapy with a willingness to work on your life situation, and an openness to change.

• Don't expect a therapist to "give" you the answers. The best professional help allows you to figure things out for yourself — and to build the skills which permit you to take it from there.

It's Not Over ...

The process of growth — positive change toward your goals for your life and your relationship — ends only with the end of life itself. You can keep on becoming more attractive, communicating better, committing yourselves to each other, enjoying life more, following your purposes more faithfully, and trusting one another more throughout your lives.

You will never be problem-free in your intimate organism — it's a human system after all! But resolving problems helps keep intimacy alive and flowing and growing to new levels of development.

You'll be happier, more relaxed, more motivated, easier to get along with, more energetic, when both of you are dedicated to caring for your intimate organism. Like most things in life, by giving more to your intimate partnership, you'll gain more from it.

We hope this book has provided you with a beginning.

bibliography

Alberti, R. & Emmons, M. (1990) *Your Perfect Right: A guide to assertive living.* San Luis Obispo, CA: Impact Publishers, Inc.

Amodeo, J. & Amodeo, K. (1986) *Being Intimate.* New York: Routledge & Kegan Paul.

Bach, G. & Wyden, P. (1969) *The Intimate Enemy.* New York: Avon Books.

Bach, G. & Deutsch, R. (1970) *Pairing.* New York: Avon Books.

Barranger, Jack (1988) *Knowing When To Quit.* San Luis Obispo, CA: Impact Publishers, Inc.

Bateson, M. C. (1989) *Composing A Life.* New York: Atlantic Monthly Press.

Beck, A. (1988) *Love Is Never Enough.* New York: Harper & Row.

Benson, H., & Klipper, M. (1976) *The Relaxation Response.* New York: Avon.

Brandt, D. (1985) *Is That All There Is? Overcoming disappointment in an age of diminished expectations.* New York: Pocket Books.

Blinder, M. (1990) *Choosing Lovers.* Macomb, IL: Glenbridge Publishing, Ltd.

Brehm, S. (1985) *Intimate Relationships.* New York: Random House.

Buber, M. (1958) *I and Thou.* New York: Scribner's.

Campbell, S. (1980) *The Couple's Journey: Intimacy as a path to wholeness.* San Luis Obispo, CA: Impact Publishers, Inc.

Campbell, S. (1984) *Beyond the Power Struggle.* San Luis Obispo, CA: Impact Publishers, Inc.

Carr, J. (1988) *Crisis In Intimacy.* Pacific Grove, Ca.: Brooks/Cole.

Clinebell, C. & Clinebell, H. (1970) *Intimate Marriage.* New York: Harper & Row.

Comfort, A. (1972) *The Joy of Sex.* New York: Crown.

Cosby, W. (1989) *Love and Marriage.* New York: Doubleday.

Crowther, C.E. (1986) *Intimacy*. New York: Bantam Books

Dahms, A. (1972) *Emotional Intimacy*. Boulder, Colorado: Pruitt.

Derlega, V. & Chaikin, A. (1975) *Sharing Intimacy*. New York: Prentice-Hall.

Gottman, J.M., Notarius, C. J., Gonso, J., Markman, H. J. (1976) *A Couple's Guide to Commmunication*. Champaign, IL: Research Press.

Greenwald, J.(1975) *Creative Intimacy*. New York: Pyramid Books.

Grigg, R. (1989) *The Tao of Relationships*. New York: Bantam New Age.

Hall, G. B. (Spring/Summer 1989) Thinking ethically in a morally chaotic world. *Crossings*. Berkeley, CA: The Church Divinity School of the Pacific.

Hart, K. (1988) A requisite for employee trust: Leadership. *Psychology: A Journal of Human Behavior*, 25 (2), 1-7.

Johnson, D. W., Johnson, R. T., Holubec, E. J. & Roy, P. (1984) *Circles of Learning*. Alexandria, VA.: Association for Supervision and Curriculum Development.

Kalellis, P. (1979) *Wedded or Wedlocked?* Canfield, OH: Alba House Communications.

Keillor, G. (1989) *We Are Still Married*. New York: Hawthorne Books.

Lazarus, A. (1986) *Marital Myths: Two dozen mistaken beliefs that can ruin a marriage (or make a bad one worse)*. San Luis Obispo, CA: Impact Publishers, Inc.

Lederer, W. & Jackson, D. (1968) *The Mirages of Marriage*. New York: W.W. Norton.

Lerner, H. (1989) *The Dance of Intimacy*. New York: Harper & Row.

Mantell, M. (1988) *Don't Sweat the Small Stuff (P.S.: It's all small stuff!)* San Luis Obispo, CA: Impact Publishers, Inc.

Miller, J. (1978) *Living Systems*. New York: McGraw-Hill.

Miller, S., Nunnally, E.W. & Wackman, D.B.(1975) *Alive and Aware*. Minneapolis, MN: Interpersonal Communications Program.

Miller, S., Wackman, D., Nunnally, E. & Saline, C. (1981) *Straight Talk*. New York: Rawson Wade.

Napier, A. (1988) *The Fragile Bond*. New York: Harper & Row.

Otto, H. (1969) *More Joy in Your Marriage*. New York: Hawthorne Books.

Powell, J. (1978) *Unconditional Love*. Allen, TX: Argus Communications.

Prather, H. & Prather, G. (1988) *A Book for Couples*. New York: Doubleday.

Remple, J. & Holmes, J. (1986, Feb.) How do I trust thee? *Psychology Today*, 29-34.

Rubin, L. (1983) *Intimate Strangers*. New York: Harper & Row.

Satir, V. (1988) *The New Peoplemaking*. Menlo Park, CA: Science and Behavior Books.

Scarf, M. (1988) *Intimate Partners*. New York: Ballantine.

Smedes, L. (1988) *Caring and Commitment: Learning to live the love we promise*. New York: Harper & Row.

Solomon, R. (1988) *About Love*. New York: Simon & Schuster.

Viorst, J. (1972) *Yes, Married: A saga of love and complaint*. New York: Saturday Review Press.

Watzlawick, P. (1983) *The Situation is Hopeless, But Not Serious*. New York: W. W. Norton.

Weinstein, M. & Goodman, J. (1980) *Playfair: Everybody's guide to non-competitive play*. San Luis Obispo, CA: Impact Publishers, Inc.

Welwood, J. (1985) *Challenge of the Heart*. Boston: Shambala Publications.

Williams, R. (1989) *The Trusting Heart*. New York: Random House.

Woititz, J. (1985) *Struggle for Intimacy*. Deerfield Beach, FL: Health Communications.

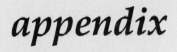

appendix

Notes for Professionals

appendix

Notes for Professionals

During the preparation, research and writing of *Accepting Each Other*, our theoretical perspective and many practical aspects of our approach have been influenced by the work of writers and researchers in several fields of inquiry:

- Intimacy Theory
- Systems Marital Therapy
- Behavioral Marital Therapy
- Cognitive-Behavioral Theory and Practice
- Marriage Preparation, Enrichment, Enhancement and Training.

This professional Appendix offers a few highlights from each of these disciplines, together with a list of resources suggested for further exploration of each. These brief therapist notes have been presented in order to illustrate some of the important concepts from the therapeutic tributaries to our thinking about intimacy. We trust that this information will stimulate your thinking about these concepts and that you will use these ideas as a springboard to practice improvement and research.

Intimacy Theory

- Intimacy as a distinct area of scholarship is a recent and undeveloped field. Formal study of intimacy started in the early 1950s, and *Psychological Abstracts* first employed the category in 1973.

- The technical definition of intimacy derives from the Latin word "intimus", meaning inner or inmost. Intimacy definitions in the popular and professional literature vary widely. Some emphasize one or two aspects of intimacy and others generate lists of many dimensions of intimacy.

• Most intimacy research is focused upon the development of intimacy within individuals across the life span, or on intimacy within marital dyads and families.

• A sizeable body of intimacy literature is devoted to the examination of "self-disclosure" as the central core of intimacy.

Resources

Acitelli, L. (1984) Marital Intimacy: Theories, values and measures. Unpublished manuscript. University of Michigan, Ann Arbor.

Acitelli, L. (1985) The influence of relationship awareness on perceived marital satisfaction and stability. Unpublished manuscript, University of Michigan, Ann Arbor.

Acitelli, L. and Duck, S. (1987) Intimacy as the Proverbial Elephant. In D. Perlman and S. Duck (Eds), *Intimate Relationships*, Newbury Park, Ca.: Sage Publications, pp. 297-308.

Amodeo, J. & Amodeo, K. (1986) *Being Intimate*. New York: Routledge & Kegan Paul.

Bach, G. & Wyden, P. (1986) *The Intimate Enemy.* New York: Avon Books.

Brehm, S. (1985) *Intimate Relationships.* New York: Random House.

Buber, M. (1958) *I and Thou.* New York: Scribner.

Carr, J. (1988) *Crisis In Intimacy.* Pacific Grove, CA: Brooks/Cole.

Clinebell, C. & Clinebell, H. (1970) *Intimate Marriage.* New York: Harper & Row.

Crowther, C.E. (1986) *Intimacy.* New York: Bantam.

Dahms, A. (1972) *Emotional Intimacy.* Boulder, Colorado: Pruitt.

Derlega, V. & Chaikin, A. (1975) *Sharing Intimacy.* New York: Prentice-Hall.

Erikson, E. (1963) *Childhood and Society.* New York: Norton.

Greenwald, J. (1975) *Creative Intimacy*. New York: Pyramid Books.

Hendricks, G. & Hendricks, K. (1985) *Centering and the Art of Intimacy*. New York: Simon & Schuster.

Malone, T. & Malone, P. (1987) *The Art of Intimacy*. New York: Simon & Schuster.

Mazur, R. (1973) *The New Intimacy*. Boston: Beacon Press.

McGill, M. (1985) *The McGill Report on Male Intimacy*. New York: Holt, Rinehart and Winston.

Olson, D.H. (1975) Intimacy and the aging family. *Realities of Aging*, College of Home Economics, University of Minnesota.

Olson, D.H. (1977) *Quest for Intimacy*. Unpublished paper, University of Minnesota.

Perlman, D. & Fehr, B. (1987) The development of intimate relationships, In D.Perlman and S. Duck (Eds), *Intimate Relationships*, Newbury Park, CA: Sage Publications, pp. 13-22.

Ramey, J. (1976) *Intimate Friendships*. New York: Prentice- Hall.

Rubin, L. (1983) *Intimate Strangers*. New York: Harper & Row.

Scarf, M. (1988) *Intimate Partners*. New York: Ballantine.

Schaefer, M. & Olson, D.H. (1981) Assessing Intimacy: The Pair Inventory. *Journal of Marital and Family Therapy*, January: 47-60.

Sloan, S. & L'Abate, L. (1985) Intimacy. In L. L'Abate (Ed), *The Handbook of Family Psychology and Therapy*, Homewood, Il.: Dorsey Press.

Waring, E., et al, (1980) Concepts of Intimacy in the General Population. *Journal of Nervous and Mental Disorders*, 68:471-474.

Waring, E. & Reddon, J. (1983) The measurement of intimacy in marriage: the Waring Intimacy Questionnaire. *Journal of Clinical Psychology, 39*: 53-57.

Waring, E. (1988) *Enhancing Marital Intimacy Through Cognitive Self-Disclosure*. New York: Brunner/Mazel.

Whitbourne, S. K. & Ebmeyer, J. B. (1990) *Identity and Intimacy in Marriage: A study of couples*. New York: Springer-Verlag.

Wynne, L. & Wynne, A. (1986) The quest for intimacy. *Journal of Marital and Family Therapy*, 12: 383-394.

Systems Marital Therapy

• Systems theory — the concept that an intimate couple or family must be viewed as an interactive system — has emerged as the central theme in the profession of marriage and family therapy. The general idea behind the systems approach to marital therapy is that the behavior of an intimate dyad is governed by (1) the qualities of each partner, (2) the interactions between the partners and (3) the impact of their environment upon them (e.g., friends, families, children). The emphasis is on the emotional transactions between the partners.

• Systems therapists generally seek to increase positive reciprocity, to decrease coercive/blaming behavior, to have couples recognize and modify dysfunctional communication patterns and rules.

• Systems theorists view the couple's life cycle as a developmental framework within which the realtionship evolves. Marital stress is seen as a failure of the system to adapt to new requirements of the couple/family life cycle (e.g., birth of a baby; empty nest syndrome).

• The roles of power and control are important concepts from a systems perspective. Therapists assess "boundaries" — lines of demarcation within the system — in an effort to learn how well partners are differentiated from each other and from other components in the system.

Resources

Angyal, A. (1941) *Foundations for a Science of Personality*. New York: The Commonwealth Fund.

Aylmer, P. (1986) Bowen family systems marital therapy. In N. Jacobson & A. Gurman (Eds.) *Handbook of Marital Therapy*, New York: Guilford Press, 107-148.

Bateson, M. C. (1989) *Composing A Life.* New York: Atlantic Monthly Press.

von Bertalanffy, L. (1968) *Organismic Psychology and Systems Theory.* Barre, Massachusetts: Clark Univ. Press

Bowen, M. (1978) *Family Theory in Clinical Prctice.* New York: Jason Aronson.

Cassirer, E. (1953-1955-1957) *The Philosophy of Symbolic Forms.* Three Volumes. New Haven: Yale University Press.

Eisenstadt, A. (1967) Language and communication in marriage counseling. In H. L. Silverman (Ed.) *Marital Counseling.* Springfield, IL.: Charles C. Thomas, 212-236.

Fiorito, B. (undated) *A Student Guide to Family Therapy.* San Luis Obispo, CA: El Corral Bookstore, California Polytechnic State University.

Gurman, A. & Kniskern, D. (1977) Enriching research on marital enrichment programs. *Journal of Marriage and Family Counseling.* 3:3-10.

Gurman, A. (1978) Contemporary marital therapies: a critique and comparative analysis of psychoanalytic, behavioral and systems theory approaches. In T.J. Paolinom Jr. and B,S, McGrady (Eds), *Marriage and Marital Therapy.* New York: Brunner/Mazel, 445-566.

Haley, J. (1976) *Problem-solving Therapy: New stategies for effective family therapy.* San Francisco: Jossey-Bass.

Hoffman, L. (1981) *Foundations of Family Therapy: A conceptual framework for systems change.* New York: Basic Books.

Kantor, D. & Lehr, W. (1975) *Inside the Family.* San Francisco: Jossey-Bass.

L'Abate, L. & Mc Henry, S. (1983) *Handbook of Marital Interventions.* New York:Grune & Stratton.

Leary, T. (1957) *Interpersonal diagnosis of personality.* New York:The Ronald Press.

Miller, J. (1978) *Living Systems.* New York: Mc Graw-Hill.

Nichols, W. C. (1988) *Marital Therapy: an integrative approach.* New York: The Guilford Press.

Reiss, (1981) *The Family's Construction of Reality*. Cambridge, MA.: Harvard University Press.

Resnikoff, F. (1981) Teaching family therapy: ten key questions for understanding the family as patient, *Journal of Marital and Family Therapy*, 14 (4):351-369.

Ruesh, J. & Bateson, G. (1951) *Communication: The Social Matrix of Psychiatry*. New York:Norton.

Sameroff, A. (1983) Developmental systems: contexts and evolution, In W. Kessen (Ed.), *Handbook of Child Psychology*, Vol. 1, New York: Wiley, pp. 237-294.

Seeman, J. (August, 1989) Toward a model of postive health. *American Psychologist*, 1099-1109.

Sluzki, C. (1983) Process, structure and world views: toward an integrated view of systemic models in family therapy. *Family Process*, 22:469-476.

Stanton, M, (1981) Marital therapy from a structural/strategic viewpoint, In G.P. Sholevar (Ed.), *Marriage is a Family Affair: A textbook of marital and family therapy*. Jamaica, New York: S.P. Medical & Scientific Books.

Steinglass, P. (1978) The conceptualization of marriage from a systems theory perspective, In T.J. Paolino and B. S. McGrady (Eds), *Marriage and Marital Therapy*. New York: Brunner/Mazel, pp. 298-365.

Sullivan, H. S. (1953) *The Interpersonal Theory of Psychiatry*. New York: Norton.

Todd, T. & Stanton, M. (1983) Research on marital and family therapy: answerw, issues and recommendations for the future. In B.B. Wolman & B. Stricker (Eds.) *Handbook of Family and Marital Therapy*, New York: Plenum.

Todd, T. (1984) Strategic approaches to marital stuckness. *Journal of Marital and Family Therapy*. 10:373-379.

Todd, T. (1986) Structural-Strategic Marital Therapy. In N. Jacobson & A. Gurman (Eds.) *Clinical Handbook of Marital Therapy*. New York: Guilford Press, 71-105.

Watzlawick, P., Bevin, J., & Jackson, D. (1967) *Pragmatics of Human Communication: A study of interactional patterns, pathologies and paradoxes.* New York: Norton.
Watzlawick, P. (1983) *The Situation is Hopeless, But Not Serious.* New York: W. W. Norton.
Werner, H. (1967) *Comparative Psychology of Mental Development.* Revised edition. New York: International Universities Press.

Behavioral Marital Therapy

* Behavioral marital therapists begin with a thorough assessment of a couple's interaction patterns, focusing on specific, observable positive and negative behaviors by each partner. Behavioral research suggests that a couple's rate of marital satisfaction is directly tied to the amount of positive reinforcement exchanged. In distressed marriages, partners reciprocate at high rates of both positive and negative behaviors.
* Behavioral treatment begins with inducing positive expectancies in both partners and developing a willingness to work together to improve the relationship. The therapist also attempts to have the couple understand the idea of equal responsibility for the creation of their current problems and conflicts.
* A wide variety of behavioral techniques are available to the therapist: behavior exchange procedures, communication training, problem solving, contracting, relaxation training, stress management, assertiveness training, homework assignments.

Resources
Alberti, R. & Emmons, M. (1976) Assertion training in marital counseling. *Journal of Marriage & Family Counseling,* 49-54.
Birchler, G. (1972) Differential patterns of instrumental affiliative behavior as a function of degree of marital distress and level of intimacy. Doctoral Dissertation, University of Oregon. *Dissertation Abstracts International.* 1973, 33 14499B-4500B, University Microfilms, NO. 73-7865,102.

Gottman, J.M., Notarius, C. J., Gonso, J., Markman, H. J. (1976) *A Couple's Guide to Commmunication.* Champaign, IL: Research Press.

Hops, H., Wills, T., Patterson, G. & Weiss, R. (1972) *Marital Interaction Coding System.* Unpublished manuscript. Oregon Research Institute.

Jacobson, N. & Margolin, G. (1979) *Marital Therapy: Strategies based on social learning and behavior exchange principles.* New York: Brunner/Mazel.

Jacobson, N. & Munroe, A. (1986) Marital Therapy: A social learning-cognitive perspective, In N. Jacobson & A. Gurman (Eds.) *Handbook of Marital Therapy.* New York: Guilford.

Kelly, G. (1955), *The Psychology of Personal Constructs, (Vol. 1).* New York: Norton.

Jacobson, N. (1990) Marital Therapy (advanced clinical seminar at Long Beach, CA). Institute for the Advancement of Human Behavior.

Knox, D. (1970) Behavior therapy and marriage problems. Paper presented at Annual Meeting of the National Council on Family Relations, Chicago.

Knox, D. (1971) *Marriage Happiness: A behavioral approach to counseling.* Champaign, IL.: Research Press.

Lazarus, A. (1971) *Behavior Therapy and Beyond.* New York: McGraw-Hill.

Liberman, R.P. (1970) Behavioral approaches to family and couple therapy. *American Journal of Orthopsychiatry,* 40: 106-118.

Patterson, G. & Hops, H. (1972) Coercion, a game for two: Intervention techniques for marital conflict. In R. E. Ulrich & P. Mountjoy (Eds) *The Experimental Analysis of Social Behavior.* New York: Appleton-Century-Crofts.

Rappaport, A. & Harrel, J. (1972) A behavioral exchange model for marital counseling. In A. S. Gurman & D. G. Rice (Eds.) *Couples in Conflict.* New York: Aronson, 258-277.

Stuart, R.B. (1969) Operant-interpersonal treatment for marital discord. *Journal of Marriage and the Family*, 37: 295-303.

Weiss, R., Hops, H., & Patterson, G. (1973) A framework for conceptualizing marital conflict, a technology for altering it, some data for evaluating it. In L. A. Hamerlynk, L. C. Handy, & E. J. Marsh (Eds.) *Behavior Change*. Champaign, IL.: Research Press.

Weiss, R., Birchler, G. & Vincent, J. (1974) Contractual models for negotiation training in marital dyads. *Journal of Marriage and the Family*, 36: 321-331.

Weiss, R. (1980) Strategic behavioral marital therapy : toward a model for assessment and intervention. In J. Vincent (Ed), *Advances in Family Intervention, Assessment and Theory (Vol 1)* Greenwich, Ct.: JAI Press.

Weiss, R. (1984) Cognitive and strategic interventions in behavioral marital therapy. In K. Hahlweg & N. Jacobson (Eds.) *Marital Interaction: Analysis and modification*. New York: Guilford, 337-355.

Weiss, R. (1984) Cognitive and behavioral measures of marital interaction. In K. Hahlweg & N. Jacobson (Eds), *Marital Interaction*, New York: Guilford.

Cognitive-Behavioral Theory and Practice

• Cognitively oriented therapists begin by assessing cognitive structures (attitudes, beliefs, self-statements, "automatic thoughts,") in order to plan appropriate interventions. Assessment can be conducted with available measuring instruments which measure thought processes generally or within specific areas: depression, assertiveness, marriage. Clinicians also conduct *in vivo* assessments through "think aloud" instructions, having clients write down their thoughts and by listening for intimations of underlying thought processes.

• Intimate partners' attitudes, beliefs, and expectations have distinct influences on their behavior toward each other and on their level of marital satisfaction. Cognitions which partners hold about themselves, about each other, about the relationship, and about their intimate environment are vital factors in determining how they get along with each other.

Resources

Abrahms, J. L. (1982) Cognitive-behavioral strategies to induce a collaborative set in distressed couples. In A. Freeman (Ed.) *Cognitive therapy with couples and groups*. New York: Plenum.

Baucom, D.H. & Epstein, N. (1990) *Cognitive-Behavioral Marital Therapy*. New York: Brunner/Mazel.

Beck, A. (1988) *Love Is Never Enough*. New York: Harper & Row.

Beck, A. (1963) Thinking and Depression: Idiosyncratic content and cognitive distortions. *Archives of General Psychiatry*, 9: 36-46.

Christensen, A. (1981) Perceptual biases in couples' reports of their own interactions. Paper presented: Association for Advancement of Behavior Therapy, Toronto.

Dodson, K. (1988) *Handbook of Cognitive-Behavioral Therapies*. New York: Guilford.

Doherty, W. J. (1981) Cognitive processes in intimate conflict: 1. Extending attribution theory. *American Journal of Family Therapy*, 9: 3-13.

Edelson, R. & Epstein, N. (1981) Cognition and marital adjustment: Development of a measure of unrealistic relationship beliefs. Paper presented: Association for Advancement of Behavior Therapy, Toronto, 1981.

Ellis, A. (1989) The history of cognition in psychotherapy. In Freeman, A., et al. (Eds.) *Comprehensive Handbook of Cognitive Therapy*. New York: Plenum Press, 5-19.

Ellis, A. (1955a) New approaches to psychotherapy techniques. *Journal of Clinical Psychology Monograph Supplement*. Brandon, Vermont, Volume 11.

Ellis, A. (1955b) Psychotherapy techniques for use with psychotics. *American Journal of Psychotherapy*, 9:452-476.

Emery, G., Hollon, S.D. & Bedrosian, R.C. (Eds.) (1981) *New Directions in Cognitive Therapy*. New York: Guilford.

Epstein, N. & Baucom, D. H. (1989) Cognitive-behavioral marital therapy. In Freeman, A., et al (Eds) *Comprehensive Handbook of Cognitive Therapy*, New York: Plenum Press, 491-513.

Freeman, A., Simon, K., Buetler, L. & Arkowitz, H. (Eds.) (1989) *Comprehensive Handbook of Cognitive Therapy*. New York: Plenum Press.

Kendall, P.C. & Braswell, L. (1985) *Cognitive-behavioral Therapy for Impulsive Children*. New York: Guilford.

Lazarus, A. (1986) *Marital Myths: Two dozen mistaken beliefs that can ruin a marriage (or make a bad one worse)*. San Luis Obispo, California: Impact Publishers, Inc.

Lester, G., Beckham, E. & Baucom, D. (1980) Implementation of behavioral marital therapy. *Journal of Marital and Family Therapy*, 189-199.

Mahoney, M. (1988) The cognitive sciences and psychotherapy: patterns in a developing relationship. In K. Dobson (Ed) *Handbook of Cognitive-Behavioral Therapies*. New York: Guilford.

Mahoney, M (1974) *Cognition and Behavior Modification*. Cambridge, Ma.: Ballinger.

Meichenbaum, D. & Goodman, J. (1971) Training impulsive children to talk to themselves. *Journal of Abnormal Psychology*, 77: 127-132.

Meichenbaum, D. (1977) *Cognitive Behavior Modification*. New York: Plenum.

Marriage Enrichment Theory and Practice

• "Marriage enrichment" programs focus primarily on preventive rather than remedial approaches. Hof and Miller (1981) indicate that marriage enrichment is centered on the following goals:

1. To increase each person's awareness of self and partner,

especially the positive aspects, strengths, and growth potential of the individuals and the marriage.

2. To increase exploration and self-disclosure of the partners' thoughts and feelings.

3. To increase mutual empathy and intimacy.

4. To develop and encourage the use of skills needed by the partners for effective communication, problem solving and conflict resolution.

Most such programs are designed for relatively healthy couples, rather than as therapeutic interventions for ailing relationships.

Resources

Hof, L. & Miller, W. R. (1981) *Marriage Enrichment Philosophy, Process and Program*. Bowie, MD: Robert Brady.

Mace, D. R. (1983) The marriage enrichment movement. In D. Mace (Ed.) *Prevention In Family Services: Approaches to family wellness*. Beverly Hills: Sage, 98-109.

Smith, L. (1983) Promoting family wellness through the churches. In D. Mace (Ed.) *Prevention In Family Services: Approaches to family wellness*. Beverly Hills: Sage, 201-213.

Worthington, E. L., Buston, B. G.& Hammonds, T. M. (1989, June) A component analysis of marriage enrichment: Information and treatment modality. *Journal of Counseling and Development*, 67: 555-560.

- There are three marital enrichment approaches on which a number of experimental research studies have been conducted: The Couple Communication Program (CCC); Premarital Relationship Enhancement Program (PREP); The Relationship Enhancement Program (RE).

- *Couple Communication Program (CCC)* — These programs were developed at the University of Minnesota Family Study Center by Sherod Miller, E. Nunnally, and D. Wackman in 1968. Wackman and Wampler (1985) indicate that the format of CCC is based on systems theory, communication theory, and a family developmental framework (families move through recognizable stages and critical role transitions take place in going from stage to stage). Six basic concepts are emphasized in CCC: awareness, rules, metacommunication, disclosure and receptivity, skills, and esteem building.

Resources

Miller, S., Nunnally, E.W. & Wackman, D.B. (1975) *Alive and Aware*. Minneapolis, MN: Interpersonal Communications Program.

Miller, S., Nunnally, E.W. & Wackman, D.B. (1978) *Minnesota Couple Communication Program*. Minneapolis, MN: Interpersonal Communications Program.

Miller, S., Nunnally, E.W. & Wackman, D.B. (1979) *Talking Together*. Minneapolis, MN: Interpersonal Communications Program.

Miller, S., Wackman, D., Nunnally, E. & Saline, C. (1981) *Straight Talk*. New York: Rawson Wade.

Wackman, D. & Wampler, K. (1985) The couple communication program. In L. l'Abate & M. Milan (Eds.) *Handbook of Social Skills*. New York: Wiley, 457-476.

Wampler, K.S. (1982) The effectiveness of the Minnesota Couple Communication Program: A Review of Research. *Journal of Marriage and Family Therapy*, 8 (3): 345-355.

• *Premarital Relationship Enhancement Program (PREP)* — Developed in 1980 by Howard Markman and Frank Floyd, the PREP approach emphasizes seven general competencies: communication and problem solving skills, the use of self-statements as discriminative cues to guide the use of communication skills, increasing perceptual accuracy, recognizing attributional tendencies or cognitive sets, development of a joint relationship world image or shared framework for the relationship, developing a sense of mastery over future problems.

The overall goals of PREP are to teach couples communication skills, problem solving skills, negotiation skills, how to deal with relationship expectations, sexual education and enhancement and to provide couples with information about relationships.

Resources

Floyd, F. & Markman, H. (1983) Observational biases in spouse interaction: toward a cognitive/behavioral model of marriage, *Journal of Consulting and Clinical Psychology.* 51: 450-457.

Markman, H, & Floyd,F. (1980) Possibilities for the prevention of marital discord: A behavioral perspective. *American Journal of Family Therapy*, 8:29-48.

Markman, H., Floyd, F., Stanley, S., & Jamieson, K. (1984) A cognitive-behavioral program for the prevention of marital and family distress: issues in program development and delivery. In K. Hahlweg & N. Jacobson (Eds), *Marital Interaction*, New York: Guilford, 396-428.

Markman, H. (1984) The longitudinal study of couples' interactions: implications for understanding. In Hahlweg, K. & Jacobson, N. (Eds), *Marital Interaction*, New York: Guilford, 253-281.

Markman, H., Floyd, F., Stanley, S. & Lewis, H. (1986) Prevention. In N. Jacobson and A. Gurman (Eds.) *Handbook of Marital Therapy.* New York: Guilford.

•*Relationship Enhancement (RE)* — Bernard Guerney is the founder of this approach, described in his 1977 book, *Relationship Enhancement*. The theoretical foundation of RE derives from four areas: psychodynamic, humanistic, behavioral, and interpersonal. The first three areas are based on current basic principles in those disciplines. The interpersonal area is based on the work of Harry Stack Sullivan (1953) and Timothy Leary (1957). Guerney (et al., 1986) adopts certain aspects and rejects others from each area and mixes them all together into an integrated format.

Nine basic skills are taught in RE: expressive; empathic; discussion/negotiation; problem and conflict resolution; self-change; helping others change; generalization-transfer; teaching supervisory (facilitative) skill; maintenance.

Resources

Collins, J. D. (1977) Experimental evaluation of a six-month Conjugal therapy and Relationship Enhancement Program. In B. G. Guerney, Jr. (Ed.) *Relationship Enhancement: skill training programs for therapy, problem prevention, and enrichment.* San Francisco: Jossey-Bass.

Ely, A., Guerney, B. G. Jr. & Stover, L. (1973) Efficacy of the training phase of conjugal therapy. *Psychotherapy: Theory, Research, and Practice.* 10 (3) 201-207.

Guerney, B. G. Jr. (1977) *Relationship Enhancement.* San Francisco: Jossey Bass.

Guerney, B. G. Jr., Brock, G. & Couful, J. (1986) Integrating marital therapy and enrichment: the relationship enhancement approach. In N. Jacobson & A. Gurman (Eds) *Clinical handbook of marital therapy.* New York: Guilford Press, 151-172.

Hardley, G. & Guerney, B. G. Jr. (1989) A Psychoeducational Approach. In Figley, C.R. (Ed.) *Treating Stress in Families.* New York: Brunner/Mazel.

Leary, T. (1957) *Interpersonal Diagnosis of Personality.* NY: Wiley.

Rappaport, A. (1976) Conjugal relationship enhancement programs. In D.H.L. Olson (Ed.) *Treating Relationships.* Lake Mills, IA: Graphic.

Sullivan, H. (1953) *The interpersonal theory of psychiatry.* New York: Norton.

General Professional References

Acitelli, L. and Duck, S. (1987), Intimacy as the Proverbial Elephant. In D. Perlman and S. Duck (Eds), *Intimate Relationships*, Newbury Park, Ca.: Sage Publications, pp. 297-308.

Clinebell, C. & Clinebell, H. (1970) *Intimate Marriage*. New York: Harper & Row.

Corey, M. & Corey, G. (1987) *Groups: Process and practice*. Pacific Grove, CA: Brooks-Cole.

Fitzpatrick, M.A. & Badzinski, D. (1985) All in the family: communication in kin relationships. In M.Knapp & G. Miller (Eds.) *Handbook of Interpersonal Communication*. Beverly Hills: Sage Publications, 687-736.

Gurman, A. (1978), Contemporary marital therapies: a critique and comparative analysis of psychoanalytic, behavioral and systems theory approaches. In T.J. Paolinom Jr. and B.S. McGrady (Eds.), *Marriage and Marital Therapy*. New York: Brunner/Mazel, 445-566.

Ivey, A. (1988) *Intentional Interviewing and Counseling*. Pacific Grove, CA: Brooks-Cole.

Jacobson, N. & Margolin, G. (1979), *Marital Therapy: Strategies based on social learning and behavior exchange principles*. New York: Brunner/Mazel.

Johnson, D. W., Johnson, R. T., Holubec, E. J. & Roy, P. (1984) *Circles of Learning*. Alexandria, VA.: Association for Supervision and Curriculum Development.

L'Abate, L. & Mc Henry, S. (1983), *Handbook of Marital Interventions*. New York: Grune & Stratton.

Malone, T. & Malone, P. (1987), *The Art of Intimacy*. New York: Simon & Schuster.

Markman, H., Floyd, F., Stanley, S. & Lewis, H. (1986), Prevention. In N. Jacobson and A. Gurman (Eds.) *Handbook of Marital Therapy*. New York: Guilford Press.

Minuchin, S. (1974) *Families and Family Therapy*. Cambridge, MA.:Harvard University Press.

Nichols, W. C. (1988), *Marital Therapy: An integrative approach.* New York: Guilford.

Perlman, D. & Fehr, B. (1987) The development of intimate relationships, In D.Perlman and S. Duck (Eds), *Intimate Relationships*, Newbury Park, Ca.: Sage'Publications, pp. 13-42.

Sloan, S. & L'Abate, L. (1985), Intimacy. In L. l'Abate (Ed), *The Handbook of Family Psychology and Therapy*, Homewood, Il.: Dorsey Press.

Whitbourne, S. K. & Ebmeyer, J. B. (1990), *Identity and Intimacy in Marriage: A study of couples*. New York: Springer-Verlag.

Wynne, L. & Wynne, A. (1986), The quest for intimacy. *Journal of Marital and Family Therapy*, 12: 383-394.

index